The House of a Thousand Memories

The House of a Thousand Memories

Growing Up in the Seventies in Sri Lanka

SUNIL TANTIRIGE

IGUANA

Copyright @ 2019 Sunil Tantirige
Published by Iguana Books
720 Bathurst Street, Suite 303
Toronto, ON M5S 2R4

All rights reserved. No part of this publication may be reproduced, stored in a retrieval system or transmitted, in any form or by any means, electronic, mechanical, recording or otherwise (except brief passages for purposes of review) without the prior permission of the author.

Publisher: Meghan Behse
Editor: Toby Keymer
Front cover design: Meghan Behse
Front and back cover photographs courtesy of Sunil Tantirige
Title page photograph courtesy of Sunil Tantirige

ISBN 978-1-77180-363-2 (paperback)
ISBN 978-1-77180-364-9 (epub)
ISBN 978-1-77180-365-6 (Kindle)

This is an original print edition of *The House of a Thousand Memories*.

Table of Contents

Prologue 1
A Walk Down Memory Lane 3
My Sister Goes for a Swim 5
Sri Lanka in the Sixties 10
Life on the Mount 15
The House of a Thousand Memories 21
Cowboys and Indians, Girls and Boys 25
Music Comes Into My Life 31
To the Stars: The Books I Read 36
Holiday Travels 41
The Southern Coast 46
Of Buddha, Angels, and Demons 50
The End of the Sixties, The End of an Era 60
Full House in the Seventies 64
Baila! 69
At the Movies 72
Ringo: One of a Kind 77
Spreading My Wings: The Seventies 80
The Young Zoologist 89
The Stuff We Ate: Ambul Thyal, Pol Sambal, and Rice 91
Of Fishermen and Lighthouse Keepers: My Parents' Story ... 99
More Than Just Six Fingers: My Sister 114
The Sun Never Sets 118
The Years of Living Dangerously: Communal Tensions 122
Me and Harry Potter's Flying Car 126
School Daze 129
Just What Did You Do for Me, Dad? 144
Coming Back Full Circle 145
Epilogue 148

To my wife Kanthi and our son Sanjay,
for the life you share with me.
And to my mother and sister, and my late father,
for the life you gave me.

Prologue

This is the story of a childhood spent on the island of Sri Lanka, where I was born and lived the first twenty-five years of my life. Then I moved to Canada to continue the university education that I had begun in Sri Lanka. The original plan was to quickly complete my graduate work in engineering at the University of Toronto and get back to Sri Lanka as soon as possible. However, the best laid plans always seem to get upended in life. A couple of years after my arrival in Canada, Kanthi, my then girlfriend and now wife, also moved to Toronto. We had met at the University of Moratuwa in Sri Lanka and got married while we were still graduate students at the University of Toronto. When our studies were complete, we decided to stay and make Canada our home. A few years later our son was born, and now we have lived in Canada longer than we have lived in Sri Lanka. That is the story of my life in 200 words or less. What follows are the details of the first part, those early years in my home country.

  The writing of this story was primarily driven by a desire to ensure my island experiences and tales will not be lost and forgotten after my time. These are the footprints of my existence on this planet. In the last few years I have watched in sadness as my mother has slowly descended into the netherworld of Alzheimer's and dementia. She was once a great storyteller herself who told us many tales when we were young. Now she lives with my sister in Sri Lanka with a jumbled memory, her life story forgotten, not really knowing where or who she is. She does not remember who her loved ones are. It is a sad end to a life well lived.

I also feel a strong urge to write these stories of my childhood so that our son Sanjay will have something to hold on to. Reflecting on my experiences with my late father and my ailing mother, I remember how they loved telling stories about their early lives. We had great dinner table conversations about them. At that time they were just interesting conversations. My father passed away almost twenty years ago and now my mother has no coherent memory left. Those almost-forgotten dinner conversations have taken on much more importance than just being interesting stories.

My wish is that Sanjay will hold on to these stories of mine the same way I have remembered the ones that my father and mother told us. I hope that within these stories are little nuggets that will let him understand better where his dad comes from and what makes his dad the way he is. I hope in these stories he will find some answers to his often-repeated question, "Why are you so weird, Dad?" or to his exclamation, "You and Mom, you two are such nerds!"

This is not an autobiography. Nor is it a detailed record of the Sri Lankan society in the sixties and seventies. This is a collection of stories of a child growing up in what was an enchanted land. Some of the details may not be written exactly as they happened as I have taken some literary licence to tell this tale, but they are all essentially true; I simply do not have the imagination to invent any of this. There are stories and experiences from that period that I have not included here for various reasons. I wanted this book to be about things that I look back on with fondness and nostalgia. It does not mean that I had a perfect childhood. Far from it. This is a celebration of a life that has been good to me and I want to remember those times as such.

We are all the sum total of our experiences.

A Walk Down Memory Lane

It is August 2018. I am in Sri Lanka for a short visit with my wife and our son. I am walking along a road in Mount Lavinia, a quiet residential suburb of Colombo, Sri Lanka's capital. It is a small lane really, a paved road with rows of comfortable-looking houses on either side protected by tall walls. It is the evening and the street is deserted, except for an occasional man or woman heading home after the day's work, or a car or motorbike slowly gliding past me.

The sun has gone down, and it is dark on the street except for patches of light from street lamps. The western sky still has a whiff of red to it from the sun that has just set. I am walking slowly down the street soaking in the atmosphere. At the top of the street, a signpost says "Gothami Mavatha", meaning "Gothami Lane" in Sinhala.

It is a typical Sri Lankan west coast evening. It is oppressively hot, and there is no wind. The humidity wraps around me like a wet blanket. It is quiet, but there are the night sounds that you always hear in a tropical land: frogs, crickets, and other creatures of the night singing loudly as they wake up and get ready for their nocturnal activities. There are faint sounds of a TV or radio coming from one of the houses. Looking up, I see fruit bats streaking above, searching for tasty eats for their dinner. There are no clouds, and much further up and away, stars are slowly lighting up. The Milky Way is stretched across the sky, and directly overhead I recognize the familiar sight of Orion, the hunter.

All this used to be very familiar to me, usually taken for granted. This evening I am soaking in the quiet atmosphere. These days I live in a far-off place on the other side of the world. I am here for the memories from my past.

I lived on this street many years ago. I arrived here as a small child almost forty years ago and left as a young adult some twenty years later. The houses along the road are where my friends used to live. Now the houses are hidden behind tall walls. It was not like this when we were young kids. In those days, everything was open. All the houses had low walls, or chain-link fences with hedgerows growing along them. In those days, you could walk into any of them. How things have changed.

I come to a house with a green wall and a tall black metal gate. The name board on the gate tells me that it is Number 4. My pulse quickens, for this is the house that I grew up in. The house of a thousand memories. Now it is almost empty; it looks tired and old. The veranda that runs along the front of the house is empty of people and furniture. The tall windows that made the living room so bright and airy are all closed. Once this veranda was full of kids and full of laughter. It was a sort of neighbourhood meeting place for us kids. As I look over the gate into the garden, memories come flooding back.

Let's start from the beginning.

My Sister Goes for a Swim

I came into this world in 1955, the younger of two. My sister, Mala, is three years older than me. We are from the Sinhalese community in Sri Lanka, which constitutes the majority of the people on the island. I was born in Colombo and lived with my family in a number of different small towns all over Sri Lanka in my first five years. Those early years are hazy in my memory, like an old broken film reel. Once in a while, a snippet of an old memory will spring into my mind, and I try to catch it and pin it down in the story of my life.[*]

At the time I was born, our family was living in the small town of Gampaha, close to Colombo. Then we moved to Matale, in the mountains near the town of Kandy. From there we moved to the southern coastal town of Ambalangoda, near Galle. The next move was to Negombo, a small fishing town north of Colombo, near the present-day international airport. My father, who was working for the government in the Education Service, which looked after the schools, was transferred every couple of years, and the family moved with him every time.

I don't have much memory of those early years. My mother and grandmother used to say that I cried non-stop

---

[*] If I were to write this story in a linear fashion, I would start by describing my family. However, I wanted to tell this tale in a slightly unconventional manner, so the details of my parents and my sister will follow after they have made many apperances in this tale.

for the first three months of my life. Perhaps all that screaming is how my love of music and singing got started. I know that when I was around three years old, I survived an attack of the deadly disease of polio without too much damage. That was when we were living in Ambalangoda, in the south. I was very lucky. I received timely Western treatment from a doctor who had just been trained on the disease in the UK, and then received long-term care from a Buddhist priest specializing in Eastern, Ayurvedic medicine. The combination of Western and Eastern treatments managed to get me well without any major muscle damage, except some weakening of my right leg muscles. I still walk with a slight limp. The only major permanent damage seems to have been to the psyche of my mother, who for years insisted that I should be careful with hard physical activities that would tax my leg muscles.

As my father was an enthusiastic photographer, we have lots of old photos and albums from those times. There is one faded photo of the family taken when I must have been about two years old. It was taken at a family picnic or on a trip on a river or a lagoon. We are all in a moving fishing catamaran and my father is holding me over the edge of the boat with my feet dangling in the water. My mother is seated behind us with my sister. They are all smiling. It must have been a fun time.

Another story that I have heard from those days also happened on a family picnic. The men in our party were drinking toddy, a sweet semi-alcoholic drink distilled from the syrup of coconut trees. I saw this and demanded some of it. Apparently, I would not stop screaming until my father gave me some. My mother says that I drank a full glass, got all red in my face, and fell fast asleep for the rest of the day. I have no memory of any of this but used to get teased a lot about how I started young on my drinking career.

Searching back deep in my memory banks, one of the first things that I remember is our house in Negombo. I think this was in 1960 or 1961. We lived in a large old mansion with a huge garden. The house had no piped water and had a well at the back some distance away from it where we got the water for our daily needs. A domestic maid who worked for us would draw water from the well in a bucket and fill the tanks in the house. When we bathed, we usually went to the well.

Something happened there one weekend morning that is seared into my memory. That day my sister, my mother, the housemaid, and I went to the well to have a bath. Our father had gone to Colombo and was not expected back till late in the evening. The way we bathed at the well was that the maid or our mother would draw water from the well and pour it over our heads. Each one of us would get a specific number of buckets of water, then we would soap ourselves up, and another specific number of buckets would be poured over our heads to wash the soap off. All very scientific: an exact number of buckets, no more, no less. We had to count out the number of buckets we received. Sometimes we would negotiate and plead, "Can I have one more please?" or "How come she got two buckets more than I did?"

After we had washed ourselves, my mother and I changed out of our bathing clothes and went back to the house while my sister, who would have been around eight years old then, and the maid stayed back at the well to rinse their clothes and put them out to dry. It must not have been even five minutes gone when we hear the maid shouting, "Nona,* nona, the baby is in the well!" At a moment when the maid's attention was elsewhere, my sister had tried to draw a bucket of water herself and had slipped and fallen into the

---

* "Lady" or "madame".

well. The water level was about twenty feet below ground. My mother and I run back to the well to see my sister down in the well, floating on the surface of the water. My mother, without even thinking for a second, jumps into the well to hold my sister high with her legs braced against the wall of the well. She cannot swim, nor does she know how to float. Survival instincts and adrenaline kick in to do the right thing.

By this time, the maid's shouting had attracted the attention of some people working next door, who come rushing over and pull both my sister and mother out from the well. No one is hurt. It was a lucky escape for my sister and mother. Later, this story became a standing joke in our family circle as the day when Mala and her mom went swimming. It was not a joke to be there when it happened.

That is how I remember Negombo: a mansion and a well. I am told that I started in junior kindergarten there and that we went to school in a cart drawn by a bull. I don't remember any of that either. I remember that our house was across the road from the house of the screen idols Rukmani Devi and Eddie Jayamanne, the biggest movie stars in Sri Lanka at that time. My sister says that one day, Eddie borrowed her copy of the famous Sri Lankan children's book Madol Doova, supposedly for turning the story into a screenplay for a movie. She claims that she never got the book back, and he never made the movie.

As I said before, my father, as an officer of the Education Service that managed the schools that were under government jurisdiction, had been moving from station to station all over the country every few years. Every time he got transferred, we moved with him. In the early sixties he was transferred to a job in Colombo, and it seems that he and my mother decided that we finally were going to settle down in one place. They chose the seaside suburb of Mount Lavinia. From that point onward, whenever Father was transferred, we would stay put in "the Mount", as the place was commonly called, while he would go wherever he had to go for work and come back home on the weekends.

Most of this story happens in Mount Lavinia. The first part deals with my preteen years up to the end of the sixties. The next part is my story from the early seventies to 1980, when I left Sri Lanka for Canada. I arrived in Mount Lavinia as a small child and left the place as a young adult. Many things happened in between. They were interesting times indeed.

Sri Lanka in the Sixties

So what was life like in Sri Lanka in my early years? In the fifties and sixties, Sri Lanka was relatively prosperous. Just a few years after its independence from Britain, it was one of the most advanced third world countries in terms of human development, with well-thought-out and enlightened social policies. The governments of the day looked after the people, the country was relatively free of corruption, and offices and services mostly worked. Education was free, including university. So was health care. And this may surprise many: it was one of the first countries in the world to adopt family planning, over the intense objections of the Catholic Church. The literacy rate then (and now) was above ninety per cent for both males and females, which is again unusual for a developing country, where women tend to lag behind men. In fact, in 1960 Sri Lanka produced the first woman prime minister in the world.

Then the politicians discovered the power of racially based politics and that was the beginning of the slow descent into the madness that culminated in a thirty-year civil war. Trust the politicians to ruin a good thing.

We moved to Mount Lavinia when I was about seven years old, I think sometime in 1962. We lived in a newly created subdivision there. It was a middle-class neighbourhood, created by the government for the professionals who served in the government services to live. Initially it was for Postal Department people and hence the area was known as Post

Master's Housing Scheme; later, people from other professions also moved in. In the end, it was a mix of mostly professionals who lived in this neighbourhood. They were teachers, doctors, army officers, and, like my father, officers from the Education Service, with a smattering of business families. It was a multi-ethnic, multi-religious neighbourhood — a melting pot of Sinhalese, Tamil, Burgher,* and Malay who were Buddhist, Hindu, Christian, and Muslim in their beliefs and faiths. Almost all well-educated, English-speaking families. We all got on well with each other and were tolerant of each other's religious beliefs, exchanging good wishes and good food on days of celebration and religious significance.

People working for the government received decent salaries, and at the end of their careers they could look forward to a decent pension. They had access to loans for housing and vehicles. There was pride in serving the government. They were just one generation removed from the one that did not have proper education, health care, or decent housing. They were the generation that saw independence from colonial rule and the momentous changes that came to the country because of it.

The middle class in Sri Lanka at that time was not very wealthy, but we were comfortable. We all had our basic needs met, we never went hungry, but we never had too much of anything either. There was no TV service in Sri Lanka in the sixties, so radio was king. We did not have a phone at home, but some people on our street did, so in an emergency we always had access to one. We did not have a fridge then, which meant that my mother had to cook daily and my parents had to shop every other day as food preservation and

---

* Descendants of European men who had children with native Sri Lankan women.

storage was not easy. All the houses in the neighbourhood had piped-in water and electricity. Most people cooked in old-style wood stoves; however, we also had a modern electric stove that my mother used to bake all kinds of goodies. Every house had a car.

As kids we did not get many presents. The lucky ones among us would receive a new piece of clothing every few months. Usually girls' dresses were handmade by our mothers and aunties. I never had more than one pair of shoes at a time. Toys and books were few and hard to come by. So, we had to resort to bartering among ourselves. If I had a book that no one else had, I would barter it for the use of a friend's bicycle. One of my friends had regular access to Western comic books such as Batman and Spider-Man, so he had an exalted social status among us. We had to negotiate with him to get our hands on these, and even then at great personal cost to our few worldly possessions such as tennis balls, key chains, hats, bats, and all kinds of other knick-knacks that kids accumulate. He got wealthier and wealthier by the day and the rest of us gradually lost most of our modest possessions. Reading Mark Twain's Tom Sawyer, I could really relate to Tom stripping off the wealth of his friends who came to see him paint his fence.

One thing that our family did that was not common to other families was to travel all over the country. As part of his duties, my father was constantly visiting schools all over the island. Often, we would go with him. These road trips were fun. In addition, every few weeks or so we would pile into our car and head down south to the coastal towns of Hikkaduwa and Galle, where our grandmothers lived (by the midsixties both of my grandfathers had passed away). We looked forward to those southern trips because our grandmothers spoiled us and, these places being costal towns with nice beaches, there was always beach time for us down there.

I don't think I was ever unhappy about my life during those days. Growing up middle class in Sri Lanka, every day you saw people, especially kids, who had very little or nothing. The contrast is huge, and it is in your face. How can you complain that you have only one pair of shoes when you know that children your age are going to school barefoot? Can you complain about the food when you know that there are kids your age that only get one meal a day? As the popular Sinhala song went, "I was crying for a pair of shoes, until I saw you who did not have legs. I was crying for mascara for my eyes until I saw you who could not see."

Because ours was smaller than the average middle-class family, our parents could provide us with a little bit more in comforts than most parents could. It was a matter of division of limited resources among a lesser number of children. For example, we went to see movies regularly with our parents. That would not be that common in a family where you had to pay for four or more kids. I received private music lessons — again, something that would be difficult to afford in a larger family.

This was a much simpler time, before TV, video games, and smart phones became necessities of life for kids. Whatever we lacked in material things was made up for by the sense of community and family we felt. We grew up surrounded by friends, cousins, uncles, aunties, and grandparents. Extended families play a huge part in Sri Lankan society even now. Every adult that we interacted with was addressed as "uncle", "aunty", "seeya" (grandfather) or "archchi" (grandmother, pronounced arch-chi). Every one of our older friends was either "ayya" or "akka", meaning big brother or big sister. Anybody younger than us was either "malli" (little bro) or "nangi" (little sis).

However, don't get the idea that it was a perfect world. The country had enough problems to go around. There was a lot of poverty and political unrest at times. It was a very unequal society. In addition, ethnic tension between Sinhalese and Tamil people was slowly building up throughout the sixties and seventies. Then we had our own personal ups and downs, heartbreaks, and disappointments. However, when I look back, the positives outweigh the negatives. So, I would like to think that I had an enchanted childhood. When you have lots of good memories it is easy to forget the bad ones.

Life on the Mount

Mount Lavinia in the sixties was a sleepy southern suburb of Colombo, its claim to fame being its beautiful beach and the world-famous Mount Lavinia Hotel that is right on the beach. This is the only safely swimmable beach in the Colombo area, and people come from all over the city on weekends to hang out, go for a swim, and have a relaxing time. It is a wide expanse of golden sand, bordered by the railway tracks that run parallel to the beach, separating it from the residential areas. The town of Mount Lavinia is on a small hillock above the beach area. When you look north from the hotel and the beach, you can see all the way to downtown Colombo, about twelve kilometres away. The west-facing beach is known for its stunning sunsets.

Travelling from Colombo to Galle on the main road leading south, you hit Mount Lavinia immediately after leaving the city. In the sixties it was a just a collection of small shops, bus and train stations, and a collection of nondescript government and commercial buildings. If you turned right onto Station Road at the main junction, you would go past the bus station, the post office, and a bunch of hole-in-the-wall type shops, and the road drops toward the beach where the Mount Lavinia Hotel and the train station are located. If you turned left at the junction and travelled along Templers Road for about a kilometre or two, you would come to the area that we lived in. In the sixties this was a new subdivision, carved out from an old rubber plantation that was no longer being worked. Being in an old plantation, our neighbourhood was still surrounded by tall rubber trees, some more than fifty feet tall. The houses there were laid down in a rectangular grid pattern along streets parallel to Templers Road and connected to it by two perpendicular streets, one at each end. Gothami Mavatha, the street that we lived on, is the middle one of three parallel streets. In those days the streets were not paved; they were just gravel roads with potholes that became small ponds during the monsoon.

Each house on the street had a plot of land surrounding it. In the front gardens we grew flowers shaded by fruit trees, while vegetable patches and banana trees were in the backyards. Every house and its plot of land was delineated from the others by low brick walls or chain-link or barbed wire fences with hedgerows. These were all modern houses, built in the sixties. With running water and electricity, they were comfortable, middle-class dwellings.

Each house and its occupants had different things going on. In addition to having regular jobs, they had "side shows". One family had chickens in their backyard, and we bought eggs from them. Another house had a plant nursery where they sold roses. People from all over came to buy rose bushes from them. One family, at the very end of our street, had connections abroad, so they had all kinds of hard-to-get foreign goods like cameras and electronic gadgets for sale. This was at the time when the country had strict import restrictions, and as a result foreign goods were hard to come by. Just outside this area there were a bunch of small shops where you could get the basic daily needs of a household. The mail, newspapers, bread, milk, and fresh fish were delivered right to your doorstep. For your major shopping needs, you had to visit one of the more commercial suburbs of Colombo, just north of Mount Lavinia. On Sunday mornings, Station Road at the Mount Junction would be blocked off for an open-air market where you could buy most household items such as spices, rice, vegetables, fruit, and fish.

Mount Lavinia today is totally different from the place that we moved to in the sixties. The inexorable expansion of Colombo in all directions has swallowed the once-sleepy suburban town. It now has supermarkets, banks, restaurants, grocery and specialty clothing stores — pretty much everything that residents in that area need. Many apartment buildings and condominiums are going up. They still hold the Sunday open market at the Mount Junction. In the beach area, in addition to the grand old lady of the Mount Lavinia Hotel, there are many small hotels and guest houses for tourists. The road that goes inland to our area, Templers Road, is now a major route connecting Mount Lavinia to the southeastern suburbs of Colombo, where Kotte, the administrative capital of Sri Lanka, is located with the parliament and government offices.

The immediate area of Gothami Mavatha is still relatively unchanged. The lanes are all paved now, and most of the previously single-storey houses have been expanded to become two storeys tall. The walls surrounding the gardens are higher and more secure. Security concerns and progress have come to my old neighbourhood. Everyone now lives behind tall walls and locked gates. However, it is still the same leafy neighbourhood that we grew up in.

When we learned that we were moving to Mount Lavinia, my sister and I were thrilled. It was a pretty nice and safe neighbourhood. We were especially happy because after living in small towns in old-style houses and mansions far from Colombo, we were moving to the big city, into a modern flat[*] with a modern kitchen, a modern pantry, and a

---

[*] Apartments are called "flats" in Sri Lanka, just as they are in the United Kingdom.

modern attached bathroom. Having a modern bathroom was a big thing for me because I hated the detached outhouses of the old houses, away from the main house — dark, smelly, and full of cobwebs. I had a pathological fear of spiders then. The new flat also meant that we had an indoor shower with a bathtub! No more going to the backyard well for a wash.

I still remember going to see the flat that we were going to live in for the first time. It was the upstairs part of a big new two-storey house with a garden all the way around. I was blown away to see how different it was from all the places we had lived before. One of the old mansions we had lived in before even had a reputation of being haunted! Our parents, not wanting to scare us, didn't tell us about these rumours until long after we had left that house. But there were definitely no ghosts in the new flat. I remember my mother saying to the owners who were showing us around, "Our son is going to be really happy here". She never knew how much!

The day we moved in, we had driven from Negombo with a truck following us with all our possessions. The first thing I noticed was four kids around our ages, three boys and a girl, looking on from the house across the road. *Good, I thought, we are going to have friends just across from us.* And indeed, in no time we became fast friends. The six of us are now scattered across the world, with only one boy from that family and my sister remaining in Mount Lavinia. We are still friends. Out of the three boys, one had some developmental issues. His name was Dayan. He had a speech impediment and a hearing deficit from birth. Dayan became my absolute best friend. We were basically inseparable during those early years. It still amazes me that both he and I accepted each other so unconditionally. His difficulties with speech and hearing posed no problems to our interactions. We did not have any hang-ups of one being superior to the other; we were kindred spirits. How friendships can grow when they are allowed to do so without any hindrances from others, especially from adults!

To me, Dayan did not have problems. He was just slightly different in the way he spoke. I just had to make sure that he understood what I was saying, and that I understood what he was saying. We were there to get along and, by God, get along we did. I did not realize it then, but soon, without even knowing, we were lip-reading each other so that one of us could understand what the other was saying just by watching his lips move. We had overcome his speech and hearing impediments, just like that. I remember his mother jokingly saying, "Dayan can't hear us when we shout at him across the table, but he can perfectly understand when Sunil moves his lips from his house across the road!"

Dayan was good with his hands in terms of building stuff, and I always liked to do things like that. Together we would build all kinds of things: model airplanes, ships, models of machinery, simple electric circuits. He was also physically strong and was always the best at any game we played in the neighbourhood. He was so fast compared to the rest of us that we called him Ruhunu Kumari, the name of the express train that ran past Mount Lavinia to the south of the island. He was and still is a gentle soul. To this day he works as an engineering draftsman in Colombo.

Once, many years later, I had gone back to Sri Lanka for a visit and went to see Dayan, still living at the same house on Gothami Mavatha. By this time, all his siblings had moved out of the country and his father had passed away. He was there looking after his mother, now very old and with dementia. I sensed that he was lonely. During our conversation he told me, "You have now a nice family, a nice boy, a nice job, live in a nice country. I have nothing and no one. I only have a small job. I did not get married because my parents did not want me to. They feared that I will have problems in raising a family with my difficulties. They were scared that others will exploit me. All because I could not speak properly and could not hear properly." All this he told me in the strange dialect that only he and I knew and understood. I was gutted. I hope he did not see the tears that I desperately tried to hide while we kept talking. Why is life so unfair?

Gradually our neighbourhood group of kids started to grow. I don't know exactly why (maybe because we had six kids in the two houses), but most other kids on the road came to our houses to gather and hang out after school. This was our playground where we played cops and robbers and road cricket. This was where we learned to ride bikes. These were the gardens where we first climbed trees. This was where we understood that kids come in all different shapes, forms, and types. Some are leaders, some followers; some adventurous, some timid; some straight as an arrow, honest, some who will bend the truth. There was one boy who could not bear to lose at anything when we played, so the rest of the kids banded together to make sure he lost a lot!

The House of a Thousand Memories

After a few years of living in the flat, my parents decided that they wanted to put down our roots in this neighbourhood. So, Father bought a vacant plot of land close to the flat, got a loan from the government, and built a house for us. The layout of the house he planned himself, with input from our mother. Us kids got rooms to ourselves, an unheard-of thing in the middle-class Sri Lanka of the time, where the average family had more than two kids, more likely four or five. I even got an attached bathroom! The house was airy and full of light, with large living areas and tall windows all around. A long veranda that ran the full length of the house at the front became a sort of gathering place for local kids. I loved that house — the house of a thousand memories.

Because the new house was being built two plots down from the flat that we lived in, I saw it being constructed from the ground up. This was in 1964. Every day after school I would run to the building site and watch masons and carpenters at work. I was there when the first foundations were cut, and I was there when the final doors and windows were hung to complete the house. By the time it was ready, I knew every inch of the house from top to bottom and every corner of the garden.

In the small plots of land at the front and in the back, my father planted many fruit trees: mango, guava, rose apple (jambu), avocado, banana, and king coconut (thambili). It was a veritable orchard. Over the years we had lots of fruit from this garden, and there were times when we supplied lots of fruit to our neighbours too. There were many types of tropical flowers growing there also: anthurium, rose, bougainvillea, and all kinds of orchids. Some of the happiest times in my life were spent on and under those fruit trees eating freshly picked mangos or guavas.

I used to keep tropical fish like goldfish, mollies, and guppies in my own handmade fish tanks built out of cement panels and glass, and I was constantly trying out new aquatic plants and different types of fish. We always had a dog in our house, and cats generally moved in uninvited and settled in comfortably. Cats and dogs were always welcome as they would keep away the mice and rats. They were also good sentries against snakes. Occasionally we would hear a terrible racket in one corner of the garden and look over to see that a cat or the dog had cornered a snake. Mostly these were harmless rat snakes, but there was always the possibility that a poisonous cobra or a viper could have crept into the garden.

What was also interesting was that we had a well in the backyard, just like at our house in Negombo. Years later, we would often use it to wash rather than the indoor bathroom with the shower. We felt that water from the well was much better and felt fresher than what came through the pipes. Give people choices and it can be strange what they will settle for.

Our neighbourhood was considered safe for us boys, and as long as we were within predefined boundaries our parents really did not care where we were. They knew that we could be found in one of many houses down our street or in a backyard in the neighbourhood. During school vacations we would roam around, leaving our homes in the mornings and returning only when we were hungry or when it was the evening. All that was for the boys; the girls were much more strictly supervised, and our parents had to know where the girls were at all times. They were not allowed to roam around the neighbourhood as we did.

Just outside our area, there were extensive wetlands. The Attidiya Wetlands were fascinating to visit: part marsh, part swamp, and part rice paddy and vegetable field. The wetlands were full of birds and other interesting creatures such as water monitors, small rodents, turtles, and harmless water snakes. We were not supposed to be there, but we went all the time. We would wade in the small ponds and streams, trying to catch guppies or frogs. I think this is one place where I really developed my love of nature and the environment, the other place being the beaches down south. If our parents, especially my mom, had known that we were wandering in the wetlands, there would have been hell to pay! I don't think my father would have minded, having had similar experiences when he was growing up, but my mother, who had been brought up in an extremely sheltered household, would have been appalled and horrified.

One of the reasons for my mother's concern was that, just beyond the wetlands, there was an area of low-income houses and shacks. This area, known as Badowita, had a reputation for crime and was considered a haunt of the Sri Lankan underworld. So, clearly, if we went to the marsh, we would then wander into Badowita, that area full of "undesirables". If we went there, she reasoned, we would meet the bad guys and get exposed to all the vice in the world, and in no time we would be card-carrying members of the murderous criminal gangs. One could not find fault with her perfect logic.

We wandered in those marshes many times, exploring the absolutely fascinating nature around us, and somehow we never ran into any bad guys, nor did we get recruited to the Sri Lankan underworld, and we always came back safe and unscathed. Moreover, I came back with an appreciation of nature.

I am sorry to say that these days the Attidiya marshes are being gradually filled and opened for development. Every time we go back now, I notice new housing being constructed on reclaimed land. These developments are terrible from an environmental perspective, because in addition to being a captivating place of nature, the marshes act like a flood barrier for the whole area, soaking up rain water during the monsoon and gradually releasing that water into the rivers. If you remove that natural sponge, flooding issues in this area are sure to get bad.

Cowboys and Indians, Girls and Boys

What games did we play then? Just like present-day Canadian kids playing hockey in the street, we played road cricket. Cops and Robbers and Cowboys and Indians were always popular. Yes, I know, we don't say that anymore, but those were very politically incorrect days. This was the midsixties when John Wayne, Yul Brynner, Charles Bronson and the rest of Hollywood ruled cinema screens all over the world. Clint Eastwood and Sean Connery were new up-and-comers. One thing I remember is that, in those days, having no real idea of who the cowboys were and what they did to the Native Americans, we did not have any preference of who played on which side. Oh, the beauty and innocence of a naïve mind! One day I would be a sheriff, packing my own Colt .45 that I had cut from a piece of plywood. Another day I would be an Indian chief, galloping like crazy on a tree trunk and firing homemade arrows from a homemade bow, teaching those palefaces a thing or two.

I remember one time a friend and I were using a handsaw to cut handgun shapes from a thick piece of plywood. Suddenly the saw slipped and nearly took a toe off my foot. The two of us bandagd the wound but told no one, especially our parents. The amount of minor cuts, bruises, and scrapes we sustained during that time was endless, and we wore them like badges of honour. If someone had not fallen off a bike at least once, we did not consider him to be a true bike rider.

Having been brought up on a steady dose of sixties and seventies British World War II comics, we would fight those great battles in our yards, or, from one of our roofs, we would pilot B-17s over Germany, defying Luftwaffe fighters. Imagination ran riot.

Lots of the games that we played then, and how we played them, would be considered highly inappropriate now. If our kids were making fake guns or weapons out of wood or plastic and using them for play, I am sure we would have heard from someone — a neighbour, a teacher, or even maybe a childcare worker, in no time. We parents and our kids would be subjected to all kinds of assessments and evaluations, and one would not be surprised if a child psychologist somewhere declared that we were raising a bunch of potential murderers, gang members, war criminals, or worse. But we all ended up as pretty normal people working as engineers, doctors, accountants, and civil servants. The kids who did none of these, who had no imagination, ended up as politicians robbing the country blind!

Sometimes when I see our son at his Xbox happily banging away at monsters in Halo and at bad guys in Call of Duty, I wonder if he is doing the same thing that I did, but on a more sophisticated level.

With a large group of kids around, cliques and bands were being formed and dissolved constantly. Alliances were made and broken regularly. Arguments, taunting, and disputes were all resolved among us; no one went to the parents for dispute resolution. If the behaviour of a kid became unacceptable to the rest, street justice would be swiftly applied, and he or she would change or be shunned.

We also played many card games and board games. Most of the time these took place at our house in the front veranda. These were riotous affairs with all kinds of shouting, trash-talking and ribbing. Snakes & Ladders, Ludo, Monopoly… the list went on and on.

In those preteen days of our lives there was no separation of girls and boys. We hung out together and played together. As we transitioned into teenagers, the separation gradually began. I could hear it in my house, my mother saying to my sister that she should not be hanging out with boys of her age because she was now a "big girl". These were the same boys that she had grown up with. In my still-preteen innocence, I could not figure that out one bit. Then came my "duties". I had to chaperone my sister everywhere she went. This was serious because now it was cutting into quality time with my friends!

"Why do I have to do this?" I used to wail. "Why can't she just go by herself?"

"Because she just can't."

"She's an idiot who can't even go some place by herself!"

My sister, who was listening to all this, would retort, "Who needs you! I can look after myself pretty well." Then I would go and complain to my friends, "I can't come today, I'm on security detail for my sis." They would look sympathetically and nod their heads. "Yes, we know, life is definitely not fair. Deal with it."

Then, a few years later, my father and mother let her go to Moscow to study at the university there for five years! She was just eighteen and all on her own. Up to that time she had never stayed a night outside the house without the family. I remember asking my mom, "How come you don't want me to go to Russia with her?"

One exception to the strictures on my sister and the other girls came when we neighbourhood kids would stage variety shows. These were usually a collection of songs, dance routines, and comedy skits. It was the girls who did all the planning and the work, my sister usually being one of the lead organizers. They selected the acts to present and did the heavy lifting of planning, designing costumes, scheduling rehearsal times, organizing the after-party — generally everything that went into staging a show. We boys were told what to do, what to wear, how to act, and to make sure to be on time for the rehearsals. This was one instance where in a usually male-dominated society, we males had absolutely no say in the matter.

Mothers were press-ganged into making costumes and snacks for the after-party. Somebody's garage was the stage, with the audience seated in the driveway. The parents were required to attend the concert with no excuses entertained. The planning and rehearsals would go for weeks, usually in the evenings. On the day of the concert, the stage (the garage) would be prepared, a curtain hung, and we would go around the neighbourhood collecting chairs from the nearby houses so the audience could sit.

The show would get going in the evening with great fanfare and, with our usual luck, gradually fall apart with the stage curtain falling down at one point or someone's costume falling apart mid-performance, to the great amusement of the audience. After the performances were over everybody would go into the house and enjoy the snacks and drinks, which were strictly non-alcoholic. At the end of the evening we would disperse happily, having been entertained and well fed. My only regret is that no one took any photos of these affairs; it was not a time of cellphones with cameras.

Much later it dawned on me why my sister and the girls had so much interest in staging these shows. As teenage girls in a conservative society, they had much less opportunity for getting together and having fun. Rehearsals were the perfect excuse to be out late in the evenings at someone's house. "Have you done your homework?" "No, I will do it after the rehearsals. Do you want me to look like a fool at the concert?"

I think in time our parents wised up to the whole scheme, and gradually the shows came to an end.

As years went by our interest in activities changed. Cricket became the most important thing in our boyhood lives. Generally, we played, thought about, and lived cricket. We went to school early so that we could play cricket before the bell. We played during school recess (intervals, as we called them). We played after school. Then we went home, had something to eat, and went out and played cricket again till it was too dark to see the ball.

Mount Lavinia in general, and our neighborhood in particular, was a hotbed of cricket those days. Two former national team captains, Anura Tennekoon and Aravinda De Silva, came from our neighborhood and both lived in the area when they attended high school. In addition, Roy Dias, who was a world-class player in the national team in the eighties, was also from our neighbourhood. I remember at least one road cricket game where he was present. In later years, when he was playing for Sri Lanka, his then captain and good friend Duleep Mendis was also a common sight in our neighbourhood. I did not know any of these individuals personally; the only time I would have talked to them would have been when we exchanged pleasantries on a cricket field, but we followed their careers from the start when they were playing in the school teams and then as they moved on to club play and finally to the national team. These were the superstars of world cricket, instantly recognized and acknowledged all over the world in cricket-playing countries. In addition to these national players, there was a host of cricketers who lived in our neighborhood and played in their respective school teams at that time. So, we grew up in an environment soaked in cricket.

In our preteen years, we were not allowed to go to the real playing fields that were a bit further away from our houses because "that is where big boys play, and they use bad words". This was my mother, hell-bent on raising us without a cuss word being heard until we were thirty and married. So, we played on the road in front of our houses. There was no question of using a proper leather ball, so we played with tennis balls. If we had used a proper cricket ball, there would have been no window left intact on our road. Playing on the road, there was no opportunity to play shots on either side, as the ball would end up in somebody's garden. So we became very good at playing straight and front. If a plant or flower pot was damaged, we were sure to be in trouble.

The house next door to ours was where an old postmaster couple lived, their kids having finished school and left home. We did not understand at that time, but we were a noisy lot while playing, and we must have driven them crazy with our incessant noise. Each time one of us hit the ball into their garden it was a disaster, as they would come out and give us a good piece of their mind. If we were particularly noisy or too many balls ended up in their garden, a complaint was sure to go to our parents too. So we made a rule: hitting the ball into their garden was an automatic out for the batsman.

Music Comes Into My Life

Music has been a very important part of my life since I was small. I really must be grateful to my parents for getting me into music. I started taking violin lessons when I was probably around seven or eight years old. I don't think I was really interested at the beginning. One day, out of the blue, my father tells me, "You are going to learn the violin, we have found you a teacher who will come to our house once a week to teach you." At that time I did not exactly have a burning desire to learn the violin. I just shrugged my shoulders and said, "OK, whatever". In those days, our parents set up stuff for us, and we just obeyed. Compare that to my dealings with our son today, where every conversation seems to end with, "I don't have to do anything just because you say so, I'll do it if I think it is right and if I like it."

And that is how I became a violin player. Initially I did not like it that much. There was too much practice involved, which was cutting into more important pursuits such as hanging out with my friends and playing cricket. In addition, no other neighbourhood boy was taking music lessons and I felt it made me stand out. But it was my parents' wish and I just went along with it. They saw to it that I practised daily. I had a wonderful music teacher, who, by the way, was an uncle of the famous Sri Lankan radio personality Vijaya Corea. An amazing musician who was a treat to listen to, he also had an encyclopedic knowledge of Western classical musicians. He had all kinds of interesting stories about people like Mozart,

Beethoven, and Strauss. Gradually, I began to enjoy my music education.

As my music lessons progressed, I started to appreciate Western classical music. What I gradually realized was that the Sinhala pop melodies I had been exposed to up to that point have many connections to the Western music that I was learning. In reality there is no definitive boundary between Eastern and Western music. At least in the Sri Lankan context, there is almost a seamless transition from one to the other. What I also realized was that music is a universal language that cuts across borders and that you don't have to be of a specific nationality or ethnicity to enjoy the music of a specific country or culture. I could love the music of Pandith Amaradeva or Ravi Shankar and at the same time go to a different dimension with Mozart, Beethoven, and Bach. As a non-Christian, I could still feel the beauty and emotions of "Silent Night", whether it was sung in English or in German.

This love I developed for a wide range of music continues to this day. One of the advantages of living in a cosmopolitan city like Toronto is that you get exposed to many cultures of the world. If you go through the music collection that I have on my phone, you will find Eastern classical music, Sri Lankan pop, Bollywood, Western pop, rock, jazz, country, and Western classical music — quite a range. Also in my collection is the music of many countries that my family and I have visited in our travels in recent times.

Mr. Corea was a man of the old school. He absolutely hated modern music like pop, rock, and even jazz. Occasionally I would ask him if we could play some modern music; he would turn up his nose and say, "Why do you want to play that rubbish?" One day after a lesson, I played a record of classical, instrumental arrangements of Beatles tunes without telling him what they were. I remember that they included songs like "Yesterday" and "Hey Jude". He listened and asked me what this music was. You could see that he was interested, and it seemed he liked what he was listening to. When I told him it was The Beatles, he was very surprised and lost interest. Till he learned what it was, he liked it, and once he knew it was modern pop, he did not. Another old dog refusing to learn new tricks, I suppose.

How I got into my school orchestra is another interesting story. I was studying at Thurstan College in Colombo then — this was in Grade 7. Having had private lessons at home for a couple of years, I could handle the violin in a decent manner, although I still was not what I would call "good". My music teacher at Thurstan, Mr. Yogananda, knew I was taking private lessons and wanted me to play in the school orchestra. I did not want to, as that would have meant staying after regular school hours for practice. So, I came up with this story that my parents did not want me to play in the orchestra because they thought it would interfere with my studies. He bought the story and did not say too much more about it.

This state of affairs lasted a few months until my father ran into Mr. Yogananda somewhere in Colombo. Because my father worked in the Education Service, they knew each other. Mr. Yogananda asked why my father did not want me to join the school orchestra. My father's reply was, "What? We never said such a thing. Of course he will play!" That was that. The cat was out of the bag. The next day I was playing in the school orchestra.

That was the start of an amazing experience in my life. Sometimes you have to be dragged kicking and screaming into things, but you end up loving them. I was one of the few in the orchestra that could read Western music and play Eastern ragas, which are patterns of notes for improvisation that form the basis of Indian classical music. That helped me to pick up the music quickly, and suddenly I realized that I did like playing in the orchestra. I really enjoyed my time there, and I must say that we were good. In fact, we were so good that we became the all-island inter-school champions that year and were invited to take part in the massive Education Centenary Celebrations that were held the next year to mark 100 years of formal education in Sri Lanka. Our orchestra had not even played together for one year.

One of my fellow violinists was Kalana Perera. He is now one of the premier music composers and producers in the country. He has written music for film, played in the major orchestras in the country, and regularly plays backup for the top classical Sinhalese singers. I am so happy for him — someone who started his musical journey with me, now occupying such a lofty position in the music industry. Decades later I was at a concert held in Toronto by a prominent Sri Lankan singer, Sunil Edirisingha. He had a small orchestra backing him up, and it was Kalana who was playing the violin! At the intermission I went backstage to see if he would recognize me. He did at once and we spent a few minutes talking, catching up and reminiscing about the old days at the college. That was an unexpected and pleasant reunion.

Those days, being able to afford private music lessons was a rare privilege, so practically none of my friends in the neighbourhood played any musical instrument. Because no one else was doing music, I had this idea in the back of my mind that it was an "unmanly" thing to do, even if I liked it. In my mind, strong men (and boys) played sports and not violins. I had this fear that my friends would think less of me because I played a musical instrument. Little did I know.

When the time came to start my engineering studies at the university, I decided to end the music lessons. By then, I had been taking private violin lessons for more than ten years. At the same time my music teacher also said it was time to stop the lessons. "I don't have anything else to teach you", he said. So, I stopped. It was the end of an era for me.

When my friends heard that I had stopped the music lessons they said it was too bad. I was mystified by their response. I told them I always had concerns or "secret shame" because I thought they laughed at me behind my back for being a violinist. Real guys played cricket and rugby, not music!

"What? Are you nuts? We thought you were special because you are the only one in our group that could do something like that!"

"That's crazy. Why didn't you guys tell me that?"

"Ha ha, you think that we were going to ever tell you that you were special? Fat chance, violin boy." Life is strange. Don't just assume things. Sometimes you are dead wrong.

Decades later all this came to a head. It was 2008, and I was in Rome with my wife and son on a tour of Italy. One night we were at the Trevi Fountain. In the piazza in front of the fountain a guy was singing classics, songs like "'O Sole Mio", "La Paloma", "Torna a Sorriento", and a host of others. It was amazingly beautiful and haunting, giving me a feeling of melancholy. Then all of a sudden it hit me: I know these songs. I played these songs when I was young. The feeling was so surreal. Here I was, sitting in a beautiful piazza in Rome on a warm evening surrounded by people from all over the world, listening to a guy singing songs that I used to play on my violin all those years ago. I quietly said a prayer under my breath to my then late father who had started all this for me. "Thanks, Dad, you should have been here with me. I hope you are watching."

To the Stars: The Books I Read

Reading and books have played a very important role in my life. I cannot remember a time when our house did not have books. They were as important to me and my sister as food, clothing, and shelter.

Obviously, I started reading in my mother tongue, which is Sinhala. Unfortunately, there are only so many books in Sinhala that are published every year, and you quickly run out of books to read. If you wanted to read about science, travel, and a host of other topics, there were simply no Sinhala books. So, the next obvious step was to move on to English books. In Sri Lanka every student is taught English as a subject from Grade 1 to Grade 10, so everyone there has some basic understanding of the language. Not all can speak and write English, but most can understand it when it's spoken. The radio at that time had dedicated English channels. More importantly, the cricket commentaries were all in English. If you followed cricket, you had to be able to read and understand English.

In those days there was a set pattern that kids took when it came to reading English. If you were a boy, you started with comics such as Spider-Man and Superman from the Marvel and DC universes. If you were a girl, you usually started off with the books written by Enid Blyton, an English author hugely popular in Sri Lanka in the sixties and seventies. These were stories about English school kids, their school lives, their vacations and adventures, and the shenanigans that they got into. From these, you graduated to books like The Hardy Boys and mysteries and crime stories by Agatha Christie and James Hadley Chase. The Tintin comics were also wildly popular in Sri Lanka, along with Asterix and Peanuts. These were also great starters for learning to read English. Peanuts has a special place in my heart because of Linus, who is totally my mirror image — in more ways than one!

The few books we had were read and reread over and over and borrowed endlessly in the neighbourhood until they fell apart. We talked about them all the time. The biggest fights that we had in our household were when we fought with our parents to buy books. As I said earlier, books were as essential to us as food.

My first exposure to English books were the Brer Rabbit stories that my mother would read aloud and explain to me. This was before I could read English. It was a favourite nighttime activity of mine just before going to bed. I can still remember rolling on the bed laughing as Mom explained what Brer Rabbit, Brer Fox, and Brer Bear were up to in the forest. She would also interpret the comic strips that appeared in Sunday English newspapers for us. Tintin, Blondie, and Jiggs and Maggie are the ones that I remember. My sister says that every Sunday morning we would eagerly wait for the newspaper and bug our mother to interpret the comic strips for us. These were my sister's and my first introduction to English.

My first foray into English reading on my own was when I started going through comics like Superman and Batman, and British war comics such as Battle Cry and Commando. These were picture books with detailed artwork that told stories from World War II. I was really interested in World War II and devoured these as soon as I got my hands on them.

Our parents were dead set against us reading comics, which they called trash. The conventional wisdom among the parents was that we would ruin our English by reading these comics. I suppose nothing less than Dickens, Austen, and Shakespeare was good enough for them. They did not realize that people who started on this trash would soon upgrade their reading to more substantial stuff.

Given that one cannot go that far reading only comics or picture books, I had to progress to real books. By this time my sister, who was deep into Enid Blyton stories, was going on incessantly about the Famous Five, the Secret Seven, and Malory Towers. So, I decided to see what the fuss was about, picked up a book, and got hooked. That was my introduction to reading English books, a habit that I have never given up. I still read one or two books every week, mostly e-books that I borrow from the library.

Books have opened an amazing world for me. With books I have gone all over the planet without leaving the house. I have gone hunting man-eating tigers in the foothills of the Himalayas with Jim Corbett, climbed to the summit of Everest with Jon Krakauer, flown night-bombing raids over Berlin with Len Deighton, and chased Russian spies all over the world with John Le Carré. I have explored Indian cities with Rohinton Mistry and stepped inside Tutankhamen's burial chamber in the Valley of the Kings with Howard Carter.

I went to Machu Picchu with Hiram Bingham years before I ever set foot there. I was on the summit of Mauna Kea in Hawaii, in the shadow of the giant telescopes probing the universe, long before I stood up there physically with my wife and our son. So, if I never get to walk on the Silk Road, stand with the Terracotta Warriors of Xi'an, or swim in the waters off the Galapagos Islands, I will still be happy in the knowledge that I have done all these things in my mind. It would be safe to say that if I was given the choice of nice food or books with just cheese and crackers, I would definitely settle for the books and crackers.

A few years after I started reading English, I stumbled upon science fiction. The main driver was that in 1968 the movie 2001: A Space Odyssey opened in Colombo. My father took all of us to see the movie, and it blew my mind. So, this is what scientists and engineers did! I think my first steps to an engineering career were taken that day at the Majestic Cinema in Colombo. You hear that many famous scientists, astronauts, and engineers were inspired by science fiction that they read when they were young. Well, you can add this not-so-famous engineer to the list.

Following that introduction to science fiction, I devoured books by authors like Arthur C. Clarke (who wrote 2001), Isaac Asimov, Larry Niven, and Carl Sagan. Clarke lived in Colombo and so I was fortunate enough to be able to see and listen to him live at a number of science- and film-related gatherings there. In fact, around 1972 or '73, I saw 2001 for the second time at a special screening at the Colombo Film Society. Clarke was there to introduce the movie and there was a lively question and answer session after the screening. Then I saw that movie for a third time a few years ago in Toronto when the Toronto International Film Festival had a special screening, and I took our son to it. To my dismay, he did not enjoy the film at all! Today's kids, absolutely no appreciation for things that were culturally significant to us then.

In the late seventies, Clarke was appointed as the chancellor of my university, and in 1979 I had the absolute pleasure and honour of receiving my degree in chemical engineering from him at our convocation. My only claim to have met and interacted with a real-life celebrity! I wish I could have told him that he played a small part in my becoming an engineer.

In July 1969, I listened on the radio to Neil Armstrong as he walked on the moon and uttered those famous words,

"One small step for a man..." There was no TV in Sri Lanka at that time. I was pretty bummed out about that. Men were walking on the moon, and I couldn't watch it live.

I can still remember making cardboard models of Apollo 11's Saturn V rocket, scouring books and newspapers for details. I had a scrapbook full of pictures of planes, rockets, trains, and ships cut out from magazines and newspapers. In a small, third world country, far off from Cape Canaveral, an engineer was being slowly cooked. Years later, when I had a chance to visit Kennedy Space Center in Florida, walk under the giant Saturn V rocket there and sit at the old Apollo Control Center watching a simulation of the Apollo 11 moon landing, life seemed to have reached some sort of a milestone in a process that started many years ago in a Colombo cinema.

It was at this same time in the late sixties that I joined the British Council Library in Colombo. With its extensive collection of books, I was in heaven. I would go there every week, get the three books that you were allowed to borrow at one time, rush home, and try to read them as fast as possible. There I went through authors such as P. G. Wodehouse, C. S. Forester, Alistair MacLean, W. E. Johns (of Biggles fame), and Ian Fleming, with relish. I also read through their extensive collection of nature and astronomy books.

Holiday Travels

One thing that our family did differently than most other middle-class families in Sri Lanka was that we travelled. We did not travel outside the country, but we certainly travelled a lot inside. As our father did so extensively throughout the country for work, often we would go with him, especially if it was during school vacations. By the time we were teens we had seen many places across the country. That is how I got the travel bug.

Our extended family was spread throughout the southern parts of the island. When we went somewhere, in most major towns or cities on the southern coast we could find a friend or a relative to stay with. In those days there were very few hotels in these towns and there was no tradition of staying at a hotel when you went somewhere. Dropping in at someone else's house unannounced was the norm, and you were always welcome no matter when you showed up.

It was a different time, when women stayed at home and had lots of help in terms of servants and maids. Unannounced guests were not a huge problem. Now the situation is entirely different. With both spouses usually working and with all kinds of after-school activities for the kids, and with cellphones in everyone's hand, no one will visit unannounced. This is a lifestyle that is gone forever.

With my father working for the government, he had access to inexpensive travel warrants on the railways and even on the domestic airline. We took many long train journeys and did several air trips to far-off places on the island.

One such trip that I still vaguely remember was to Jaffna in the far north of the country. It was around 1964–65. Jaffna is the capital of the Tamil-speaking minority area of the country. My father had some school-related work there and it was school vacation time, so we joined him on the trip. We flew to Jaffna in an old Air Ceylon DC3, which I was certain had taken part in World War II air campaigns. We came back on the train, the night mail to Colombo. We stayed in the small town of Chunnakam with a schoolteacher friend of my father's.

If you look on a map, Sri Lanka is the pear- or teardrop-shaped island hanging just under India to the east of the subcontinent. At the top of the island there is a small peninsula shaped like a bird's head, attached to the rest of the country by a narrow strip of land. This is Jaffna Peninsula. Historically this area has been populated by Tamils, who are the largest minority group of the island. The climate there is totally different from the rest of the island, very arid, with Palmyra palms instead of the coconut palms that are found in the rest of the country.

Jaffna was also the centre of the Tamil opposition to the central government, which was led by the majority Sinhalese. It is where Tamil militancy got started and the demands for a separate state grew in the sixties. By the midseventies, tensions were slowly increasing between Sinhalese and Tamil communities, and Jaffna Peninsula was gradually cut off to Sinhalese as hostilities took off. From the mid-1980s to 2009 this area would be the major battle ground in the civil war. By the time the war ended the whole area had been devastated, a once vibrant and hard-working community decimated, and a significant portion of the Tamil population had been displaced and were living in other countries where they had fled from the war.

The things we do to each other under the guise of nationalism, ethnic identity, unity, language, and religion. I once read something online that said, "Cataracts are the third biggest cause of blindness. Religion and politics remain the first two." We in Sri Lanka have proved that many times over.

However, all that still lay in the future when we made our family trip to Jaffna in the midsixties. I don't remember much of the trip, except that there were some kids my age there who I played cricket with, me without knowing a word of Tamil and them not knowing a word of Sinhala, and neither party speaking any English to communicate with the other. We got on fine. I think there is a message of sorts there to the two communities that in the next thirty to forty years tried their best to kill each other.

I also remember on that trip that we visited Nagadeepa, the famous Buddhist temple on an island off the Jaffna coast. You had to take a short boat ride from the mainland to reach this tiny island. We also went to the baths at Keerimalai hot springs and visited Tholagatti Farm at the Rosarian Monastery in Atchuvely,* where Christian monks sold Nelli Crush, a bittersweet drink made from local berries. For the first time I ate idli, which is a South Indian Tamil food, a type of savoury rice cake that you eat with a curry or a spicy gravy called sambar. It was also our first introduction to Palmyra sprout, or Kotta Kilangu, as they are known in Sri Lanka. These are Palmyra palm seeds, hard and crunchy. They are also known as the sprit of Jaffna. Any southerners who travelled in north brought some with them when they returned home.

One day I would love to go back to Jaffna and retrace that childhood trip. I have a feeling that it would be an emotional experience for me.

I remember that during the same period we also flew to Trincomalee, Batticaloa, and Amparai on vacations. They are

---

* My Tamil friends in Toronto tell me that this operation is still going strong, having survived the war years.

all towns on the east coast, far from Colombo. On the trip to Trinco, we took off in a storm and flew through bad weather all the way. The rickety old DC3 of Air Ceylon was being tossed like a leaf in the bad weather and at one point was leaking rainwater through the ceiling. My sister was crying in fear, but I was too young to be scared. You can't fear things that you do not know about. The fact that we could crash did not even enter my mind.

Out of these places on the east coast I remember Amparai very well. My father was stationed there in the late sixties, and we spent about two weeks with him during a school vacation. We spent the time exploring the area and saw lots of wildlife, many types of animals and thousands and thousands of all kinds of birds.

Amparai, which was a tiny village to begin with, had been developed to be a major town in the east in the fifties when the government created a huge water irrigation and agriculture project in the area. A massive reservoir had been built there by damming a river and creating large areas of agricultural land in the surrounding area. All this straight from land that had previously been a thick jungle.

Amparai was the administrative centre for the area with lots of small farming villages around it. In the sixties the area still had a very frontier feel to it, towns and villages surrounded by jungle full of animals such as elephants, deer, leopards, bears, and wild buffalo. The forest that surrounds the new reservoir is now one of the major national parks on the island.

Other than the wildlife, this area was also part of the ancient Lankan kingdom dating back more than 2,000 years and has extensive archaeological ruins, most of which were completely covered in jungle and still unexplored in the sixties. One such place that I clearly remember is Rajagala, a tall, jungle-covered mountain that towers over the surrounding plain. A few years before we were there, extensive ruins had been discovered. When we were there the ruins were being gradually exposed. There were remnants of palaces, Buddhist temples, and many ancient stone inscriptions and guard stones indicating that an extensive building complex existed on this mountain 2,000 years ago in the times when Buddhism was first introduced to Sri Lanka.

The Southern Coast

While the trips to far-off places like Jaffna and Trinco were once-in-a-lifetime events, our trips down south were regular like clockwork. Every couple of months, our parents would announce that the next day we would be going to visit our grandmothers in Hikkaduwa and Galle. We would hardly sleep those nights in anticipation.

Early the next morning we would set out in our car. The coastal road from Colombo to Galle and points further south runs right by the beach for most of the way and has some spectacular scenery. Unfortunately, these days the new expressway from Colombo to Galle and Matara runs inland from the coast and misses out on the beautiful beach scenery. Our first stop was usually in Hikkaduwa at my father's childhood home where his mom and some of his then unmarried sisters lived. We would spend a few hours there, sometimes go to Hikkaduwa Beach, and would then proceed to my mom's childhood home in Galle. By this time, both our grandfathers had passed away.

Hikkaduwa and Galle are the places where my love of the sea began. Hikkaduwa, with its protected beach and the famous coral reef, was the perfect place for a small kid to get introduced to the sea. My father's childhood home was not far from the beach, and he and his brothers had practically grown up on it. When I first came to Hikkaduwa Beach all those years ago it was still pristine, with just one small hotel, the famous Coral Gardens Hotel. The reef is just a few metres into the water from the beach and is full of coral and fish. I could not swim then, so my father would swim out to the coral reef with me hanging on to his arm. It was a picture-postcard place: blue sky, turquoise sea, a wall of coconut trees on the land, miles and miles of golden sand stretching into the horizon with the fishing catamarans lined up just out of the water. How could anyone not love that place? Many years later, we found a similar beach in Akumal, Mexico, on the other side of the world. On that beach I introduced our son to the pleasures of snorkelling over a breathtaking coral reef, just as my father did for me at Hikkaduwa.

Hikkaduwa is still around, and is still a nice place, but much of the sixties charm is gone. It is now one of the major tourist centres on the island. The beach hotels there now stretch for miles, with accompanying restaurants and souvenir shops. The fishing catamarans are all gone, replaced by diesel fishing boats and glass-bottomed boats for reef viewing. The smell of diesel fumes is ever persistent, and the reef is only a pale comparison of its past glory. The boat operators compete aggressively for clients and sometimes can be overly persistent. The relaxed atmosphere that I first experience there has almost vanished. Oh, the price of development and fame.

Galle is where my mother's parents lived. It is the third-largest city in Sri Lanka and is the administrative capital of the south. It has historical significance: it is here, in the early 1500s, that the Portuguese began the colonial conquest and rule of Sri Lanka, which lasted almost 450 years by the successive colonial powers of the Portuguese, Dutch, and English. Galle was also the principal port on the island during the Portuguese and Dutch periods until the British made Colombo the capital and commercial centre of the island in early 1800s. The Portuguese built the first fort in Galle and then the Dutch expanded it to be the massive structure that is there now. It is one of the best-preserved and "living" forts in the world and is an integral part of the city, where people live, work, go to school, and pray. It is now one of the premier tourist destinations in the country. It is also a UNESCO World Heritage Site.

Very close to my mother's childhood home was the Galle Bay with its beautiful beach. In those days it was a fantastic stretch of golden sand that went on from the old fort at the north end of the beach to the low hills of Roomassala at the southern end. This beach was also where the fishing catamarans would come and land their catches. Every morning, local people waited for the boats to arrive and bought fish directly from the boats. Whenever we were in Galle, we would just walk to the beach to relax.

Then in the late sixties, the government of the time, in its infinite wisdom, decided to build a fishery harbour there. All the houses near the beach were taken over, people moved out, and all structures were demolished. The almost endless, perfectly golden, sandy beach, was dredged and walled off, and an ugly harbour was built. It was short-sightedness of epic proportions and a crime against the people of the area. No one at that time objected. No one understood the value of a pristine beach over an ugly harbour. If that stretch of beach was there now, the place would have been heaven for tourism, both for local and foreign vacationers.

Fortunately, despite successive governments' misguided intentions, spectacular beaches are still dotted all around Sri Lanka. Even these days you can still find yourself on a stunning beach, miles and miles of golden sand and blue seas with no one else but you. Hopefully most of them will remain like that forever and not become crammed with wall-to-wall beach hotels.

On these trips to the south, we would occasionally proceed further south from Galle, visiting other relatives in our extended family. At least once a year we would go right down to Kataragama in the southeast corner of the island where there is an important Hindu temple that millions of Sri Lankans go for worship and for currying favours from the god Skanda who is supposed to reside there.

Sometimes we would also stop at Dondra Head, the southernmost point in Sri Lanka. There is a lighthouse there, and my mother lived at the lighthouse for some time just before she married my father. More about that later.

Of Buddha, Angels, and Demons

Our family is Buddhist, as the majority of Sri Lankans are. We were brought up well versed in Buddhist traditions and practices, but my parents were not diehard followers of the religion. We were taught Buddhism at school and at home, we went to the temple on important days, and throughout our lives we have been involved with all kinds of Buddhist rituals and celebrations, as part of our family and at our schools.

But my parents never forced the religion on us. We were neither asked nor expected to attend the Sunday schools many Sri Lankan kids had to go to. We were never forced to take part in whole-day "sil"* programs at the temple that many Buddhists take part in on full moon days. Buddhism for us was almost a background soundtrack to our daily lives, always present but never interfering. When we gradually transitioned into our teen years, we were allowed to question, probe, and figure out the meaning of religion for ourselves. Later in my teen years, I remember having raging debates about Buddhism with my cousins. Having said that, one wonders what my parents' reaction would have been if one morning I had announced that I had found Jesus and that from that point I was following His teachings.

---

* A "sil" at a Buddhist temple is a set of religious activities that usually takes place on full moon days. The activities involve listening to sermons by the priests, chanting, and participating in worship. They start early and go throughout the whole day.

Sri Lanka is a country where about seventy per cent of the population is Buddhist. People practice Theravada Buddhism there. The next most practiced religion is Hinduism, followed by Christianity and Islam. Most of us Sinhalese are Buddhists, but there are Sinhalese who are Christian as well. Similarly, most Tamils are Hindu, but a fair portion of the Tamil population is Christian. The Muslim community also has different groups: the Malay Muslims who originally arrived from Southeast Asia and the Arab traders who came from the Middle East and Africa and settled on the island. The common Sinhala term for Muslim is "Marakkala", which means "boatman" or "seafarer" and originates from Tamil. To complicate matters even further, while the majority of the Christians are Roman Catholics, other Christian denominations such as Anglicans, Baptists, and most other variations of Christianity are all present and active on the island. This is the result of colonial powers of different Christian persuasions occupying the island at different times. Sri Lanka is a real mix of major religions of the world.

We Buddhists are a practical lot. Most Buddhists will pray and give offerings to the gods of other religions as well as their own. They see no contradiction in that. It is common for Buddhists to pray at Hindu temples and to go to prominent Christian churches when they are facing troubles in life or need special favours from the divine. Buddhism does not forbid its followers from following other religions. Hence, the practical-minded Sri Lankan Buddhists hedge their bets by offering prayers and tribute to other gods. Let's cover all our bases, just in case!

Most Buddhist temples in Sri Lanka have at least a small place for the Hindu gods on their premises. It is a funny and uncomfortable contradiction that most Buddhists have no rational answer for, as Buddhism does not acknowledge the existence of superior beings that can bring you salvation.

Buddha preached that the ultimate salvation is within you and not granted to you by an almighty divine god. There are other contradictions, such as eating meat while the number one rule or precept in Buddhism is "thou shall not kill or take any life". Ask any Buddhist about these and he or she will jump through hoops to come up with rational answers.

Among many celebrations the country has, there are two important ones every year for Sinhalese Buddhists. One is Wesak, which is the day when we celebrate important milestones in Buddha's life such as his birth. This falls on the full moon day of May. In addition to the religious observances and poojas (religious ceremonies) that take place on Wesak, every Buddhist house will have paper lanterns lit in the evening. These are handmade and are of all shapes and colours, lit by candles that are placed inside them. Wesak evening is one of the most spectacularly enchanting times in Sri Lanka. Every Buddhist house or business establishment is decorated and lit with multicoloured lanterns.

When we were young, building these Wesak lanterns was one of the biggest highlights of each year. Just like North American kids waited for Halloween, we waited for Wesak to come around. We planned our lanterns weeks ahead. We collected the bamboo sticks to make the frames and bought the semi-transparent coloured paper to go on the frames. The paper would shine in different colours when lit by candles from inside. There was always intense competition among friends to build the most beautiful and unique lantern in the area. On the Wesak evening after we came back from the temple, we would light our lanterns and then walk around to see which house had the best decorations. At night we also lit sparklers and sent up fireworks. Some of the happiest memories of my childhood were on these occasions.

May is also the time that the monsoon commences on the west coast. There were years when it rained heavily on

Wesak night and the decorations that we put our heart and soul into were washed away. On those years we would say sadly, "Buddha is not pleased with us this year". Then again, in line with Buddhism which teaches that everything is impermanent, we did not feel bad for long. There was always the next year.

The other big celebration for us was the Sinhalese (and Tamil) New Year. Based on the old Eastern calendar and the zodiac signs, the New Year is always on the thirteenth or fourteenth of April. Each year the astrologers figured out the exact date and the time. This is not a religious festival but more like a harvest festival with some religious elements. For two days the country would come to a standstill as people celebrated the coming of a new year, with food, games, and fun activities. Every town or village had New Year festivals of sports and music. It was a time for families to be together, pay respect to the elders, and visit relatives. For the young kids it was an exciting time as we always got new clothes for the New Year. Every home had lots of special food prepared, and on New Year's Day we would light firecrackers, play, and eat the whole day. We also gave out a portion of the specially prepared food to all our neighbours, especially to the households that were not celebrating the festival, such as the Muslim and Christian households. When they held their celebrations like the end of Ramadan or Christmas, they reciprocated the gesture and we received plates of watalappan, a delicious pudding specially made by the Muslims, or Christmas cake from the Christian houses.

When one speaks of religion and rituals in Sri Lanka, one must also talk about ghosts, devils, demons, and other such nasties. Then there are the exorcisms, fire-walking ceremonies, and other similar rituals, which are the responses of the local population to those nasties. Most of these have largely disappeared now as a result of a better understanding of the environments that people live in, advances in medical knowledge, or simply because of the prohibitive cost of staging these rituals. In the sixties and seventies, however, these were still front and centre in Sri Lankan society. Now these rituals and performances are mainly staged as cultural and folklore activities performed by professional dance troops, mostly for the benefit of tourists and visitors to the island.

The good and evil beings of Sri Lanka's spiritual domain are known as "devas" and "yakshas" (literally, angels and demons). Back in the day, when sciences were not as developed as now, most things in the environment were ascribed to the moods of the good guys and the baddies of the spiritual realm. People thought that most environmental factors such as rain, floods, cyclones, droughts, poor harvests, contagious diseases, and much more were all caused by unhappy devas. So what was the remedy? You staged deva poojas, or offerings to devas, asked for forgiveness for anything that people may have done to make the angels unhappy, and tried to placate them. The astrologers determined which angel, or deva, was angry or upset. Similarly, without the availability of modern medical knowledge or diagnostic tools, people suffering from a major disease like cancer or an organ failure were thought to be afflicted by the action of a demon. Epileptic fits, depression, mental illness — these were all caused by demons possessing the patient. This is where exorcism and fire-walking rituals came in. You had to chase away the demons. You could never placate them. On the other hand, you asked forgiveness from devas. These beliefs predate most major religions such as Buddhism and Christianity and have connections to Hinduism and shamanism. However, the arrival of major religions on the island did not make these go away; they just adapted and intertwined with the new belief systems.

What is written above is not a detailed description of the spiritual and religious practices of Sri Lankan society, but is meant to give some context to what we experienced as kids growing up. When we were young we had many opportunities to attend and watch these ceremonies. In the sixties, exorcisms were very common in my Grandma's town of Galle and its outlying villages. These were all-night ceremonies involving chanting, drumming, and dancing in elaborate costumes. The costumes, with devil masks and their wearers dancing with lit torches to heavy drumbeats, could be scary. When we were small, we were usually not allowed to go and watch these, the excuses being, "You kids are too small to go, you will be scared" and "You can't stay up the whole night." So we begged, cried, and on occasion even threw temper tantrums to be allowed to go. Sometimes we were even successful. I remember going to one exorcism that was staged at the house next to my grandma's house in Galle. Halfway through the "show" I was so scared that I begged to be taken home.

Exorcism ceremonies have almost totally disappeared from Sri Lanka now. As medical science advanced, people realized that devils or demons do not cause ailments and you did not have to drive away demons using song and dance. These rituals are now part of cultural shows. The devil masks that were once part of these rituals are now sold in souvenir shops and hang in most Sri Lankan homes.

Fire-walking was slightly different. Fire walks were not specifically performed to chase away demons but to seek blessings after a particularly trying time in the village or to seek good fortune for an upcoming period that people knew would be difficult. For example, if there had been an epidemic of disease in the area, people would get together and stage a fire walk. These were much more elaborate than an exorcism, took time to prepare, and whole communities would get involved. Hence, they were also much more expensive than your run-of-the-mill neighbourhood exorcism. According to the requirements, the fire-walkers had to be pious and refrain from eating meat and consuming alcohol for a period (usually three months) before the event, and had to follow strict lifestyle rituals up to the time of the ceremony.

Fire-walking is done after hours of dancing to infectious music with a heavy beat. I have been to fire-walking ceremonies where, after listening to the music and the beat, we spectators felt that we too could walk on the pit of red-hot wood embers that had been prepared for the fire-walkers. The music and the beat were just that hypnotic. The other fact was that most of the people in these villages did not wear footwear most of their lives and as a result had thick, roughened soles. These were the key: body adaptations and mind over matter. As a spectacle it was simply unbelievable to see. I have watched kids as young as five or six dancing across the firepit with their moms and dads. For the participants there was logic to fall back on if the fire-walking did not go according to the plan and one suffered burns: you either did not follow the pre-ceremony rituals correctly, or the sprits were angry at you and sent you a sign by burning your feet.

Fire-walking myths got busted in the late seventies when the students and professors of Colombo University Medical School conclusively proved that the ability to fire-walk had nothing to do with being pious, being a vegetarian, or not consuming alcohol. It all had to do with the thickness of the soles of one's feet, the time of contact between the embers and the sole, and the hypnotic state that you put yourself into through the music. The fire-walkers danced across the embers in such a way that part of the time their feet were not in contact with the embers.

There was at least one fire-walking ceremony near Colombo where half-drunk university students and their professor went and danced with the real fire-walkers, leading to a near-riot by the enraged villagers watching the spectacle. These "truth-seekers" literally had to run for their lives.

So, most of these hardcore superstitious rituals have now disappeared from the island society, but some remain. Some beliefs are really silly; for example, any time the national cricket team gets into an important international competition, they will be sent off with religious blessings, and, if the team gets into the finals, before the game, the whole country gets busy performing poojas at temples and blessings in churches for the team. I suppose it is an attitude of "we do believe in our players, but to be on the safe side let's remind devas that an important game is coming up." Leave no stone unturned and hedge your bets — that is the Sri Lankan way.

Sri Lanka is a superstitious country. All Buddhists and Hindus, and many Christians, have their horoscopes written when they are born. Then, throughout their lives, all important events and activities are conducted on days determined by astrologers who consult their horoscope to come up with the correct or auspicious date and time for various activities. When people get married, if it is an arranged marriage, matching horoscopes are a must. Even when the boy and girl have met by themselves and fallen in love and want to get married, parental consent will be difficult to obtain if the horoscopes do not match. If you are opening a business, moving to your newly built house, even going to the airport to go abroad to start a job or to study, you will start these activities at auspicious times set by astrologers. Even these days horoscope readers do a roaring business as people go to them for practically everything. You had to have an auspicious time for giving your infant solid food for the first time, reading to your child for the first time, piercing a little girl's ears. This list was, and continues to be, endless.

If someone fell ill or lost something valuable, one went to an astrologer to find out why and what to do. Sometimes these consultations led to hilarious situations. A few years ago, my sister lost her beloved dog. One day he simply walked out of their house, and he was gone. After weeks of searching everywhere in the area and putting up missing dog posters, in desperation she went to the local astrologer for help. The way this works is that you are not supposed to tell the astrologer why you have come. The astrologer will determine why you're there by looking you over, consulting your horoscope, and watching you perform certain specific actions that he or she asks you to do. The astrologer will start the proceedings by asking a set of clever and leading questions, and the answers given by the person seeking help will tell the astrologer why that person is there. It is also said that these astrologers have their "catchers" mingling with the people waiting and these guys will gather information on why the people are there and pass that information on to the astrologer. Sort of a local spy operation — information is power, as they say!

So my sister goes to see an astrologer about her missing dog. When she arrives, he takes a hard look at her and summons whatever divine powers he has, proclaiming, "You have come about a missing person." So far he is mostly correct, but that was a safe bet. A fair number of people that go to an astrologer go there to inquire about a loved one. My sister nods her head and says "yes". Then after a few other leading questions, he says "Don't worry, this missing person is well, he has gone abroad for a job. He will be back one day."

It was indeed comforting to know that the dog was not missing; rather, he went abroad for a job and simply forgot to write back. We were speculating, was he working as a guard dog in a rich Arab prince's compound in the Middle East, or did he join US Marines as a bomb sniffer? One never knows for sure. The only thing I know is that the dog never appeared again.

One of the biggest astrological prediction flops of all time in Sri Lanka happened in 2015 when the president of the country called for new presidential elections two years ahead of schedule because his personal astrologer predicted a massive victory. He lost the elections and had to leave office. The astrologer had to go into hiding, fearing for his personal safety.

The End of the Sixties, The End of an Era

As the sixties gradually came to an end, our lives down Gothami Mavatha were slowly changing. I was moving into the complicated world of a teenager with its associated hang-ups and issues. My sister was planning to go abroad and had applied to study in Moscow on a scholarship, and we were waiting to see if that would come to fruition. In 1967 I had moved from the primary school in Mount Lavinia to a high school in Colombo where I was expected to continue until I entered university. Those changes meant new experiences, new friends, and new places.

In the meantime, we had two new additions to our household family. One was Chan, the youngest of the three cousins from my mother's brother's family. He had come to our place during a vacation, liked our set-up very much, and refused to go home! So, the adults decided that he would stay with us and go to school in Mount Lavinia. He was a few years younger than me, so he was our little brother. My sister and I teased him a lot. The other person who came to our household at that time was the daughter of one of my aunts. Her parents had passed away years ago. Priya Akka, as we called her, was older than my sister and me. She had been brought up at our grandfather's house in Hikkaduwa after her mom passed away. She had already finished school and was working as an administration assistant at a big manufacturing facility close to our house, so it was almost inevitable that she would stay at our house.

She stayed with us for a short period until she got married and started a family.

As you can gather from these arrangements, in Sri Lanka we really took care of our extended family members. If someone needed a helping hand in life, a place to stay, a place to go to school or to work, there was always someone from the extended family who would stand up and offer help. In offering a place in our house to our cousins, we were not doing anything special. In a country that does not have much government-sponsored social assistance, it is the extended families that come forward and take care of you if there is a need.

Then in the summer of 1970, a much more unexpected visitor appeared in our household. This was Monica, our "white sister" from the United States. A few months before, my sister had come home from school in a great state of excitement. An organization called the American Field Service, or AFS for short, had come to her school to discuss and asked for volunteers for an exchange program between US and Sri Lankan high school students. They were looking for host families for US students to stay for three months. The American students were expected to attend school with a child of the hosting family. The AFS people had presented the stories and experiences of the previous years and shown slides. My sister was hooked. She pleaded with my parents that we apply to host a student. My parents had no objections and an application was made. A few weeks later, a delegation from the AFS with US Embassy program coordinators came to our house to meet us. After looking us over and talking with us they did not have any objections, and a few weeks later we were informed that an American girl would be staying at our house for three months and would be going to school with my sister. The key here was that they were not paying us to host a student. It was all voluntary and we would bear the cost of her stay in Sri Lanka. My father, in his enlightened thinking, figured that we would gain immensely by interacting with someone from outside the country.

That is how Monica, a high-school student from Yuba City, California, came to stay with us. My sister was in a state of absolute excitement. They were corresponding with each other before she came to Sri Lanka, and by the time she arrived we felt that we already knew her. She arrived, I think, in June 1970. She fit into our family like a long-lost member. She ate our food, lived our life, and did the stuff that we did. We believe that she had a great time. She went to school with my sister, taking the morning school bus from Mount Lavinia to Colombo. We had lots of fun hosting her and we travelled a bit in the country showing her around, packed like sardines in our small car.

Until moving to Canada years later I simply did not appreciate what a culture shock it must have been for her to come and stay with us. I suppose it was good in a way we didn't know any of that. Her coming over to Sri Lanka was a perfectly normal event for us. As far as we were concerned, she was another in a long line of cousins and relatives that had stayed or would stay at our place at different times. What could go wrong? Pretty much nothing.

Monica returned to the United States at the end of August of 1970, I think on the day after my sister left for Moscow. After that she and my sister maintained sporadic contact in the eighties and then we lost all contacts. Although we frequently talked about her, it looked as if she had appeared and disappeared from our lives just like that. My mother always had a soft spot in her heart for Monica. Years later, when I was talking to Mom about the time Monica was at our house, she used a very Buddhist rationalization for how and why we met her: "Monica must have been one of our family from a previous life. That is why she came to see us." I thought that was a touching way of reasoning out a pleasant and unexpected event in our family's life.

Then, several years ago, I found her again through social media and surprised her with a Facebook message. She was massively surprised to hear from me and was delighted that we had made contact again. Now we are in regular contact and she follows me and my sister and our children's activities through social media. She is married to a Spanish guy and has lived in Spain for part of her life. She is a grandmother now, just like my sister. Hopefully one day in the not too distant future, we will have a grand reunion, either in Sri Lanka or in California. Sometimes life gives you totally unexpected experiences.

Full House in the Seventies

With the beginning of the seventies, many changes had come to life on Gothami Mavatha. My sister had gone to Moscow for her university studies. Many of the Gothami Mavatha neighbourhood gang had dispersed or become differently occupied, each one of us having different interests and doing different things in life. The next ten years would be a huge shift from my first ten.

By the midseventies all three of my cousins, my mother's brother's boys, were living with us. The eldest is Asoka, who is a couple of years ahead of me, Vasantha is about my age, and Chan, the youngest, is a few years junior to me. Their father, who was a doctor, did most of his service outside Colombo in small rural centres serving small villages where things like good schools did not exist. As a result, my cousins had been in student hostels most of their school lives. Chan was already at our place and going to school in Colombo. The adults discussed things, and it was decided that Asoka and Vasantha would also come and stay with us to study in Colombo during the final couple of years of their school lives. My parents must have thought that they would be good companions for me, being close to my age. Our large house had enough space for all of us, with my sister studying in Russia.

I was feeling lonely after my sister's departure to Moscow. We always had been very close to each other, so the arrival of Asoka and Vasantha was a godsend to me. While navigating those complex teen years, what could have been better than having two boys of my age around? All our "teen issues" could be figured out among ourselves without too much interference from adults.

We discussed — and argued about — everything under the sun. During those years that we four boys lived together in our house, we formed very strong bonds. I still consider them my brothers rather than my cousins. It was a fun time, with lots of laughter, lots of jokes. Even now when we get together it is usually a riot. Jokes and old stories fly thick and fast. No one is spared; there are no sacred cows when we meet.

Hence, we had a full house in the midseventies. Four cousins were living with us, the three boys and Priya Akka. From time to time my grandmother from Galle, my mom's mother, would also stay at our house.* Plus, we had a housemaid to help my mother with the housework. Then there was Ringo, our German shepherd, the cats, and the fish! With our friends constantly coming and going, the house was always full, always with something interesting happening. As we still say, "it was a happening place".

Given the large number of people staying at our house, my mother had an efficient system of work management, and she assigned work for all of us. The housemaid was there to do the grunt work like daily cleaning chores and helping my mother in the kitchen. We were obliged to do our own chores. For example, we were expected to wash our own dishes after meals. There were no dishwashers or washing machines in the house. We were expected to do our own laundry. We were also expected to help Mom with

---

* Later, in the late seventies, my grandmother came to live in Mount Lavinia permanently. By that time my cousins had already moved out. She passed away in 1986 in Mount Lavinia.

shopping. If my father was not around to drive her, one of us drove her to the market. We helped her with gardening and running errands.

Saturday was our washing day. Asoka, Vasantha, and I would go to our well. Armed with scrubs and detergents, we would wash all our clothes for the coming week. Chan was too small for this type of work and he got an exemption. We had to wear whites at school, white shirts and white pants, so there was a lot of washing to do. Given that all three of us were doing everything together, these washing events at the well did not feel like work but time spent together with all kinds of stories, gossip, talk about politics, and, of course, jokes. Remember there was no social media then. If you wanted to socialize, you had to meet and talk!

By the midseventies, my violin lessons came to an end as I got ready to enter university. Having obtained a fairly good grounding in both Western and Eastern music, I wanted to continue my involvement with music in some fashion. I had been talking with my friends about getting a guitar. What else would you think of doing in your late teens? Playing a guitar would be a cool thing to do.

My father must have overheard this, because one day he comes home from work and calls me into the living room. A beautiful guitar is on the table. My eyes light up. He simply says, "It is for you. It is yours for getting into engineering at the university."

That was a surprise indeed. Sri Lankan parents at that time usually did not verbalize these things to their kids. We usually did not get rewarded for our academic achievements, which is not to say that our parents were not happy or proud, but certain things were understood but left unsaid. So, this gesture was a really big deal for me.

Acquiring the guitar had a big impact on my social life. It was easy to master the guitar after all the training I had with the violin; I just needed to learn the chords and finger placements on the fretboard. I took to the guitar like a fish to water.

When Sri Lankans gather for a party there is always singing. I don't know many people who did not sing, some really good and others barely holding a tune. Social singing is a big part of Sri Lankan culture. It is almost essential for a party to have someone who can accompany the singers with a guitar or a piano and someone with a pair of bongos to keep the beat. I became that guy with the guitar.

As my fame as a guitar player spread, invitations to parties grew. By this time, I had a bunch of friends, all engineering students that hung out together. Occasionally we would gather at someone's house for an evening of dinner and singing. I would be the backup and we would sing late into the night. I can still remember the songs we sang those days and even now when I hear these songs, memories come flooding back, and invariably a tear or two spring to my eyes.

Playing the guitar during those university days was a real stress reliever for me. Our daily workload was enormous. Generally, we would have lectures and labs the whole day. I would come home, take a break, and hang out a bit with my friends and, after dinner, study another three or four hours on my own. Usually, before my mother called us for dinner at 8 p.m. every night, I would be in my room practising the guitar just by myself, sometimes trying out new songs and variations, sometimes just going through chord progressions. This was my quality time.

The seventies was the time of cassette tapes and vinyl records. There were no CDs, no computers, no YouTube or streaming music services. Western pop music sheets were extremely hard to come by, restricted to a fortunate few who had connections abroad. There was no written Sinhala music. Everything we played we had to figure out ourselves after listening to the music on vinyl, a cassette, or the radio.

The earliest music that I started playing on the guitar was Sinhala pop music, and the easy-to-play three-chord songs of the early Beatles. As I gained confidence, I picked up late seventies stars such as The Eagles, John Denver, Simon & Garfunkel, and a host of other folk and pop artists. I have always liked sentimental ballads. Come to think of it now, we must have sounded awful with our thick South Asian accents singing Western songs, but we didn't care. We were not practising for American Idol. Singers from the UK like Tom Jones and Engelbert Humperdinck were very popular in Sri Lanka at that time, but we did not dare to sing them as their vocal range was far beyond what we could do! I can remember once belting out a Tom Jones song at an impromptu gathering of my friends in our garage, prompting one of my sharp-witted friends to remark, "Sounds like Tom is having real stomach trouble." There is no one crueler than your friends!

Baila!

Sri Lankan music is a strange mix of Eastern and Western rhythms. Classical Sri Lankan music is heavily based on classical Indian music. The pop music is heavily influenced by Western music with a healthy dose of Eastern rhythms. Then there is of course Sri Lankan Baila music. If you're going to talk about music in Sri Lanka, you have to talk about Baila.

This is the music of the Portuguese who occupied Lanka in the sixteenth and seventeenth centuries. The white parangi[*] devils who ate white stones (white bread) and drank blood (red wine), as the native Lankans first described them, are long gone, but their music is still wildly popular everywhere in the country. Sri Lankans knew a good thing when they heard it, even if it came from the colonial masters. The beat of Baila is infectious, and over the centuries it has been infused with jazz and spiced up with East Indian rhythms.

We play, sing, and dance Baila everywhere and at every occasion — at parties, weddings, cricket matches, the end of political meetings, and on road trips. It is also the music that has been universally accepted by all communities in Sri Lanka, by Sinhalese, Tamils, Muslims, and Burghers. To not know a Baila tune or two would be an absolute disaster

---

[*] Colloquial Sinhala term for the Portuguese, often used in a somewhat derogatory fashion.

for a young Sinhalese man and he would be deemed a social outcast. "What's wrong with the guy? Does he not know any Baila?" We all claim to be good Baila singers and even better Baila dancers, although I would say some are better than others.

Some years ago, we were at a Tamil celebration in Toronto. This was during the height of the civil war between the Sinhalese majority and the Tamil minority. Most at the party were Tamils with a small number of us Sinhalese. Everyone got on fine and after the formal events and dinner it was time for music and dancing. To my absolute surprise they started playing Sinhalese Baila music. To my even greater surprise, pretty much everyone got up and danced, including grandmas and grandpas. So, between two dances, I remark to one of the Tamil guys that I never expected to hear Sinhalese music at a Tamil party. After all, this was during the height of the war, and Toronto was a hotbed of Tamil militancy. He looks at me quizzically and asks me with a serious face, "Have you ever tried to dance to Tamil music?" and he goes on, "Not unless you are an expert in Bartha Natyam or Kathak!" (These are classical South Indian dance techniques.) At that moment I thought maybe not all is lost for our country, our two communities may even get on with each other eventually. If everything else fails, we will still have Baila to unite us.

Another incident that is still vivid in my memory was in 2009 when we were in Sri Lanka for my nephew's wedding. As usual, we were all merrily dancing away at the end of the wedding reception. Moms, dads, kids, uncles, aunties, everyone was up and shaking their hips. From the dance floor I spotted our son watching us in amazement. His mom and dad, jumping up and down and swaying to this crazy music! All his cousins were on the dance floor, doing all kinds of gyrations, while Sanjay, who is Canadian-born and raised, watched all this from the side. We beckoned him to come and join us on the dance floor, but he would not budge. I suppose there are certain things that a full-blooded Canadian man will not do, and that includes dancing Baila. I must say I felt a bit sad, seeing him being left out of a part of his heritage. Maybe one day he will get the courage to get up and dance Baila at a wedding reception, but I have a feeling that I will not live to see that day. One can only hope.

At the Movies

Living in a country starved of mass entertainment (when we were growing up, there was no TV service in the country), we loved movies. As one would think, Bollywood is huge in Sri Lanka. Now, up to the time my cousins arrived to live with us, my main interest always had been in Sri Lankan and Western music. As someone who had been trained in the violin and played in the school orchestra, I was familiar with both Western and Eastern classical music. Into this mix came Bollywood!

Asoka and Vasantha were crazy about Bollywood. They lived and breathed the Indian film scene. They are the ones who got me interested in it. They would not miss a single Bollywood movie shown in Colombo. I did not even have to go and see these movies: they would go and see them, sometimes the same movie many times over, and would give me a minute-by-minute explanation of the story, the kits, the songs, and the scenery. Although they did not speak Hindi, the main language of Bollywood, they could sing most of the songs within a few days of them being heard over the radio. I think in our family circles Vasantha has the record of seeing the movie Hathi Mere Saathi seven times.

The faces of Bollywood's legendary actors and actresses were all over Sri Lanka. Names like Raj Kapoor, Rajesh Khanna, Amitabh Bachchan, Sharmila Tagore, and Vyjayanthimala come to my mind. Sri Lanka has always had this love–hate relationship with India. We love their actors and actresses but hate their cricketers. I suppose that is because there was no competition to Bollywood personalities in Sri Lanka, while when we played cricket, we always competed with them on an equal footing. The Sri Lankan movie actors and actresses were loved as down-to-earth people, no different to us, while the Bollywood ones were seen as larger-than-life, from a far-off place of fantasy. They were as exotic and unreachable to us as aliens from an Arthur C. Clarke novel.

I still remember the Bollywood movies that I saw in the seventies and still have some of the music of those movies with me. Legendary movies like Mera Naam Joker, Sangam, Aradhana, Abhimaan, and the aforementioned Haathi Mere Saathi. Their songs are everlasting and evergreen. The music of Shankar and Jaikishan, Lakshmikant and Pyarelal, the voices of Mohammed Rafi and Lata Mangeshkar, I will never get tired of them. Every time I hear that music now, I get instantly transported back to my life with my cousins in the seventies in Mount Lavinia.

What about Sri Lankan or Sinhala movies? The film industry in Sri Lanka is diametrically opposite to what Bollywood is. Not having the resources and the audience base of Indian cinema, Sri Lankans have elected to make movies dealing with social themes and issues. So, while Bollywood makes escapist mass entertainment movies that make millions of dollars across the world, Sri Lankan cinema rakes in awards at international film festivals with gritty social drama, but the movies are almost unseen and unheard of outside the country. There are several Sri Lankan directors that are well regarded all over the world. Most notable of them is of course Lester James Peries, whose 1972 film Nidhanaya is generally ranked among the top 100 films ever made anywhere in the world.

We loved Bollywood for the escapist entertainment that its movies provided. We equally loved the Sinhala cinema that provided much food for thought, spotlighted social issues, and attacked traditional norms and beliefs. Those films provided us with endless discussions, debates, and soul-searching.

Hollywood was entirely a different kettle of fish. In those days Sri Lanka never got the major Hollywood productions when they were first released across the world. Usually it took a couple of years before they were released in the country. In fact, Star Wars, which was first released in 1977 in the West, had still not been released in Sri Lanka in 1980 when I left the country. The only exception was 2001: A Space Odyssey, which was released in Colombo at the same time as in London, New York, and Los Angeles because the author of the story and the screenplay, Arthur C. Clarke, was living in Sri Lanka.

The three biggest Hollywood stars of those days for Sri Lankan audiences were Clint Eastwood, Sean Connery, and the martial arts actor Bruce Lee. Most kids (especially the boys), were absolutely fascinated by these guys. They were tough as nails and not about to burst into a song and dance routine around a tree in a park as they took down the bad guys, as the Bollywood heroes always did. I remember that Bruce Lee's signature movie, Enter the Dragon, was shown without a break in Colombo for almost two years. An opening of a Clint Eastwood or James Bond movie in Colombo was always a big event. For weeks and months before the opening day, the boys would be talking about the film. Bragging rights went to the guys who managed to get into the first screening on the first day — the first show, as we used to call it. After seeing the movie, we would talk about it incessantly, to the great annoyance and envy of those who hadn't seen it yet.

I have been in theatres where, when either Clint Eastwood or Sean Connery appeared onscreen for the first time, the audience welcomed them with standing ovations and cheering! The power that they had over our young minds was that strong. When Enter the Dragon opened in Colombo, kids went absolutely nuts. Everyone and his dog were taking, or claiming to take, martial arts training. A good excuse for someone for avoiding something was "I have karate classes at 8 p.m., machang,* I can't come."

The other Hollywood genre that we really looked forward to was World War II movies. The sixties and seventies had some legendary war movies: The Longest Day, The Great Escape, The Train, Von Ryan's Express, Battle of Britain, and Tora! Tora! Tora! to name a few. Then there is the 1957 David Lean epic The Bridge on the River Kwai, forever associated with Sri Lanka. It was filmed on locations in Sri Lanka and the Mount Lavinia Hotel played itself as the World War II army hospital, which it was during the war. The famous bridge scenes were filmed on the Kelani River in Kitulgala in the mountains of Sri Lanka. Obviously I did not see it when it was first released, but over the years I have seen it several times.

When we were in high school, one of our favourite things to do was to sneak out before the end of classes and go to a movie with a bunch of friends. That way we could go to an early showing and get home at the same time as a normal school day or just a bit late with the excuse that we had some extra work at school or something semi-plausible like that. Why did we resort to such devious methods to just go for a movie? Because in our high school days, our movie rights were severely restricted by our parents, who thought that watching too many movies, especially these "godforsaken English movies with all kinds of violence and sex", was the first step into the darkness of hell. From there it was only a few shorts steps into smoking, drinking, and only God knew what else. Then of course there was the issue of money.

---

* Sinhala equivalent of "buddy" or "bro".

Obviously, our parents did not have lots of money to spare for us to be spending it on things like movies. So, for us it was a question of beg, borrow, or sometimes even steal a few rupees and sneak off to the movies. We would buy the cheapest tickets, the gallery seats as they were called, which were the first few rows in front of the screen, so you were guaranteed to have a stiff neck and a headache by the time the movie ended. We did not care.

Years later, when my parents were at our place in Toronto, we were talking about our school days and unexpectedly it came out how I used to sneak off from school with my friends to go to movies. I don't think my father cared too much, I am sure he would most likely have guessed what we were up to anyway, but my mother was absolutely shocked! She could not imagine her dear little son doing such dastardly deeds. So I asked my mother, "OK, I played hooky from school a few times and went to the movies. But I gained admission to university to study engineering and went on to do a master's and complete a PhD in engineering in Canada before everything was said and done. I have a good job now and I am fully providing for my family. So where did I go wrong by watching a few movies in those days?" She was baffled and had no answer. In her mind kids who did those things in their school days never ended up doing advanced studies in engineering! I don't think she ever reconciled such contradictions.

Ringo: One of a Kind

Ringo was the German shepherd that came to live with us when he was six weeks old, and he basically took over the place like he owned it for the next eleven years. He was a cute little fluffy black ball when he came, running after us all over the place. As he grew up, he turned into this big, majestic-looking dog that struck fear into the heart of anyone who did not know him.

We got him because one night someone jumped the wall into our compound and cut off a garden faucet and a length of pipe. It was just a petty theft, but at the time our father was working outside Colombo and my mom was alone in the house most of the time with Mala and me. So we decided to get a dog for protection.

Soon after he arrived, he decided that in the overall hierarchy of the household he was just below our father and mother. Everyone else was below him. We were his playmates and not the other way around. Only my mom and dad had absolute control over him.

He had the complete run of the house and the garden. He knew exactly who lived at our place and would not let anyone else come in beyond the gate. Everyone who visited us would come to the gate and rattle its lock, and the first at the gate was always Ringo. Before any visitor came through, we would have to chain Ringo down or lock him in a room.

Early in the morning he would be at the gate waiting for the newspaper man to arrive. When the guy arrived, Ringo would stand up on the gate on his hind legs and take the newspaper in his mouth and run back to our father. If Father was not home, he would wander all over the garden with the paper, with us pleading with him to drop it. Eventually he would decide that he'd done enough and would drop the paper. It was the same with the mailman. Ringo simply had to be the one to receive the mail. He heard the ring of the mailman's bicycle coming down the street long before the guy was at our property, and he would rush to the gate and wait for him. If there was no mail that day for our house and the mailman just went by, Ringo would give the guy a piece of his mind, no doubt with a few well-chosen doggie curse words.

Ringo had a fearsome reputation in our neighbourhood. His biting record included me, all three of my cousins, and a couple of my friends. In all instances we had ordered him to do something or prevented him from doing something. While he was there, we had absolute security: no one would even dream of coming into our garden or breaking into our house. With our garden having so many fruit trees, the local kids would have had a field day raiding those, if not for Ringo. We had low walls around our property, and our front door and side doors were generally left open most of the day because we knew that no one would even approach our house.

He was also this sweet dog who adored us and loved us. Every day as I came home from school or from university he would come running to the gate as soon as he heard it being opened. He would jump on me, greet me, and escort me to my room. Then as I changed, he would be half on my bed with his front paws resting on the mattress and talking to me in his dog language, probably asking me how the day went. He recognized the sound of our car and would be standing up and waiting even before the car turned on to Gothami Mavatha.

For such a big and ferocious animal, he was deathly scared of firecrackers and thunder. On days of celebrations and festivals when firecrackers were set off, Ringo would be under a bed shivering in fear. He also knew the association between firecrackers and matchboxes. Every time we had a matchbox in our hands, he would be under a bed like a flash. He also knew the Sinhala word for matchbox. You had just to say it out loud, and off he would go under a bed. We often used that to control him.

He had the same reaction to thunder. Anytime there was a thunderstorm, he would quake under a bed. He could tell hours before that one was on the way. There must be something in the environment that he could sense long before the clouds and lightning appeared. He was a living weather vane.

He was amazingly intelligent and knew many Sinhala and English words. One only had to say the word "walk" and he would run to fetch his leash and be at the gate waiting. He knew exactly when he would get his dinner. If my mother was not in the kitchen mixing up his food when the time of the day came, he would get up, go to my mom, hold her hand gently in his mouth and drag her to the kitchen.

Ringo lived with us for eleven years and passed away when I was in university. That was a very sad day. For us, he was another family member. Since then, my parents have had several dogs, but there's never been another one like Ringo.

Spreading My Wings: The Seventies

The seventies were the time when I was allowed to spread my wings. In my early years in Mount Lavinia I was not permitted to wander far from the immediate neighbourhood of Gothami Mavatha. I did not mind: there were enough kids around as we had enough places to hang out with enough things to do.

Things changed as we grew older. My cousins were living with us now, and we three boys (Chan, being younger than us, had his own group of buddies) gradually increased our area of wandering. We started to go to the local sports field for our cricket and to Mount Lavinia Beach to hang out with our friends. As a result, my circle of friends increased dramatically.

Every day after school we would gather at the sports field for a pickup game. Most of the time it was cricket but sometimes we played elle, a variation on baseball which got introduced to Sri Lanka during World War II by US troops stationed there. After the game we would sit on the grass and just chat. These days our son calls that "chilling". It was a diverse crowd in terms of what we were doing and what we planned to do in our lives. Some of us were destined for university as engineers, doctors, teachers, or accountants. One became a pilot and served with the national airline in a distinguished career, while several of my friends served as cabin crew. There was one who became a sailor and worked on various shipping lines all over the world. He would sail six months of the year and then come home and spend the other six months relaxing.

The late seventies was the time when ethnic tensions were gradually building up in the country. We the younger generation talked about it constantly. The news from the north was slowly getting worse. The views among us on what to do and how to stop the coming ethnic catastrophe were as diverse as the number of people who were discussing it. One thing we were certain about: something bad was coming our way if nothing was done. No one can claim that Sri Lanka walked into its ethnic calamity unknowingly or with its eyes clenched shut. People paid the price for not speaking up or standing up when it mattered.

There were a couple of my friends who joined the army as young Officer Cadets and fought through the thirty years of civil war. I met them again a few years ago at a get-together that one of my high school friends held for me. I was meeting them after more than forty years. I could not believe that the grizzled senior army officers in front of me were the same high school kids I knew. They had fought through battle after battle for an entire lifetime. In comparison, World War II took just six years.

To get back to our lives in the seventies, in the evenings as the sun went down, the roti carts would appear in our area. These sellers pushed a cart with all the ingredients and implements to make roti on the road. They had the premixed batter and a portable gas stove to cook. The seller would sound his bell, calling out to the houses and asking if anyone needed roti. If we boys were at the playing field when the roti guy went by, we sometimes would buy them and eat sitting on the grass. A plain roti was cheap, but you had to pay extra if you wanted an egg roti. These food carts seem to be something that has now disappeared from the neighbourhood roads of Mount Lavinia. In my recent visits back there, I have never seen them around.

The other place that we gathered in the evenings was Mount Lavinia Beach. Our neighbourhood was about two kilometres inland from it, and on some evenings a group of us would walk to the beach to hang out. The west-facing beach is famous for its spectacular sunsets, "painted sunsets" as they are called. On one end of the beach is the Mount Lavinia Hotel, in continuous operation since the late 1800s when the original building there was the British governor's out-of-town mansion. The hotel has appeared in many Western movies, and was a pit stop in The Amazing Race a few years ago.

It is surprising to think of Mount Lavinia as "out-of-town" because now the city of Colombo has spread far south of "the Mount", as we called our hometown. The famous hotel has expanded significantly since it was the governor's mansion. According to old stories, the name Mount Lavinia comes from a lady named Lavinia who lived on the small hillock just behind the mansion. It is said that she was the Governor's mistress. Apparently, there was a secret passage from the residence to her house so His Excellency could visit her in secrecy. Thus, the town became Mount Lavinia.

The Mount beach was also the place that on an occasional Sunday we would go for a swim. If our father was around and was not busy, he would also join us boys. Growing up on the coast and being on the beach at Hikkaduwa for most of his young life, Dad could swim like a fish. The Mount beach in those days was one of the few beaches in Sri Lanka that had lifeguards. It was considered a dangerous place to get into the sea as there were nasty riptides there. Every year one or two people lost their lives on that beach. Many times it had a lot to do with inexperienced swimmers getting into the water without understanding the sea conditions. Despite being a tropical island and having many rivers and thousands of lakes, it is surprising how few Sri Lankans know how to swim.

Talking about swimming and the Mount beach brings up another memory and another story. This was in 1975, and I had started my first year at the university. My friends were bugging me to celebrate this "momentous milestone", as they called my gaining admission to university. What they really meant of course was that they wanted me to pay for a few bottles of their choice of alcohol and snacks. After some bargaining and hard give-and-take, I agreed that yes, we would celebrate. Another friend who had just entered medical school also agreed to pitch in. None of our parents would allow a bunch of teenagers to get drunk at their houses, so naturally the venue was the Mount beach. We would be there after dark, so a bunch of boys drinking and partying would not stand out too much.

On the night of the "momentous milestone", the party was going strong. There was a great deal of merriment, and old and new stories. It was good to be sitting on a tropical beach, eating roti and string-hoppers (rice vermicelli) and downing shots of arrack, the local alcohol of choice. Obviously, we could not afford foreign alcohol and expensive food that we would have liked to have had on such an occasion. A good time was being had by all present. In the meantime, one of my dear friends had one drink too many. Let's call him "Alok": he is now a well-known personality in the hotel management sector in Colombo, having worked all over in the Pacific and in Australia, and has a family. There are reputations to protect here.

Suddenly, Alok decides that he wants to go for a swim. Obviously, that's not a good idea given that it's dark, the sea is rough, and this is the Mount beach, which has a bad reputation for water safety. The rest of the gang, less inebriated, says no. But he will not take no for an answer and suddenly gets up, strips, and runs into the water. We run after him, grab him, and drag him back. This happens a few times.

Let me tell you, it is not easy to hold a wet, drunk, naked man when he does not want to be held! Each time he goes in, we drag him back. In the end, the guys do what's practical: we lay him flat on the beach, and about three heavy people sit on him. He's immobilized and secure. When he realizes that he cannot move, he starts to cry, "Look Sunil, these bastards will not let me go for swim at your party!" "OK buddy, it is not a pool party", someone reminds him.

Well, he did not get to swim that night, but he lived to tell the tale.

That brings up drinking. Our household was strictly non-alcoholic. We followed the fifth precept of Buddhism to the letter: "Thou shall not take intoxicants." My father did not drink or smoke. He would on very rare occasions partake of a glass of wine or something stronger. Did he drink during his University of Ceylon days? I do not know. Whatever the case may be, we did not have alcohol in our house.

During that time, most of my friends were heavy drinkers. I was not. I did not like alcohol that much, and of course I did not have money to waste on it either. The nice thing about my group of friends was that no one forced me to drink, and no one thought less of me for not drinking. I would be at these gatherings sipping a cold drink or nursing one alcoholic drink for a couple of hours while my friends would drink away. There was no peer pressure. I am also not a smoker; I may have had one or two cigarettes in my entire life.

I also remember the night Asoka and Vasantha came home late from a party. Asoka, like me, did not drink much. Vasantha, on the other hand, had drunk quite a bit at this party and was in bad shape. We had to get him inside the house and get him to bed without our parents knowing about it.

I don't remember all the details of what happened, but somehow as I open the door to let them in, my mother, who had been sleeping, wakes up and comes out to see what the commotion is. We have to think fast and tell her that Vasantha has eaten some food containing eggs at the party and is feeling the effects (he was allergic to eggs). My mother gets angry at him for not being more careful with what he ate, but mercifully she goes back to bed without too many questions. I get them in, and Vasantha then immediately throws up in the washroom. Again, mother asks him if he's OK, to which he replies, "Yes, *Nanda*,* don't you worry." She goes back to bed; Asoka is furious at his brother; I am just plain thankful that everything is under control.

The next morning everything is relatively calm. Vasantha is recovering from a humongous hangover and does not come out of his room till late afternoon. Asoka and I are pretending that we don't know anything. My mother is complaining to me, "Look at this fellow, he simply does not take care of himself. He should have been more careful knowing that he cannot take eggs and the food at these parties contain lots of stuff that has eggs in it!" To this day she doesn't know what happened.

Now I remember the time that a neighbourhood girl sent Asoka a note, "a love letter" as we called these silly things those days, which my mother somehow got hold of. We four boys had gone away to stay at my cousins' parents house for a few days during school holidays. My mom was cleaning the bedrooms while we were away and came across the letter under his bed pillow. The girl in question was from a wealthy family who had moved to a house down the street recently. The family, prominent businessmen, had a reputation of being somewhat nasty and might not react well to one of their girls "consorting" with an ordinary middle-class boy. They did not hang out that much with the locals. This was the stuff

---

* Aunty.

that Bollywood thrived on: boy meets girl, parents are angry, families go to war! My mother's overactive imagination was running wild.

Meanwhile, we were totally unaware of the impending crisis. This was a time of few landline phones, and there were no cell phones or Internet. So, news travelled slowly or not at all. We had a great time at my cousin's house in Matara deep in the south, and came home to Mount Lavinia totally rested and happy.

Not even half an hour after our return, we are summoned to a family conference at the dinner table. Things do not look good. The offending note is dramatically produced. "What is this?" my mom demands. This is bad and we have to think fast on our feet. Here was a crisis where, depending on how we responded, men would be separated from boys. We stammer, look at each other helplessly, and try to shrug it off: "You know ... it's nothing ... the girls were walking in front of the house every evening ... we just teased them ... they must have got the wrong idea ... you are making a mountain out of a..."

In my mother's mind, a Romeo and Juliet situation was developing down Gothami Mavatha. Montagues and Capulets; blood would flow down the street in rivers — Oh, the horror! The feud would run in our families for centuries.

Well, eventually saner counsel prevailed, and in the end my mother calmed down, understanding that it was just a silly note and that they were definitely not planning to elope.

So where was our father in all of this? He sat there rather quietly, only saying the absolute minimum. I have a sneaky feeling that he was enjoying the whole drama! He, a man who had vast experiences of the society we lived in, must have realized that it was nothing. Just boys being boys and girls being girls. My mother, who had a sheltered life, overreacted.

A few days later my mother corners me. "I want to know what you knew", she demands. Like a rabbit caught in a beam of light, I plead complete ignorance. "Why do you think they tell me anything?" I ask indignantly. Of course, I knew the whole story: what happened, how it got started, the contents of that note. I was furious with Asoka for leaving the note exposed like that. It was a complete breakdown of our security protocols! Fortunately, I had family currency to spend in such situations. In my parent's eyes, I was a hard-working, conscientious student, doing my studies diligently, getting good marks, and generally staying out of trouble. So, they really had no reason to give me a hard time. Mother just gives me a hard look and walks away. That was that.

Then there is the story of my father and my hair. This was late in this time period. I was already in university going through my first year. I had let my hair grow and it reached down to my shoulders. I was not making a statement, I was not being rebellious, I just let my hair grow, simple as that. I knew my father would not be happy, but I figured, I'm in university, I am now grown up, and I can do what I want. I also knew my father and knew that one day this was going to come up.

It came up in a much unexpected way. One day he was giving a ride to one of my friends. As they were driving along and chatting, all of a sudden my friend, who should have known better, says to my dad, "Uncle, I see that you now have two daughters." Of course, he was referring to my long hair. I don't know what my father said in reply, but he was not happy.

He comes home and does not talk to me or tell me what happened, but tells my mother that he wants me to cut my hair. My mom comes and tells me, "There, your father wants you to cut your hair; he says that you are not to drive with him anywhere till you do that. Your friends are teasing him." Thanks guys, I thought. Thanks for setting me up.

There was no question that I would disobey him, so I cut my hair. We did not disobey our parents. That was the unwritten rule in Sri Lankan society those days, especially in the family circles that we were in. It may be different now. I waited one or two days, just to show him that I was not about to jump when he wanted me to, and went to a barber shop and had it cut it off completely. I went from shoulder-length hair to a crew cut.

I come home, and my father looks at me and never says a word. I suppose some things are better left unsaid.

So that was my "rebellion" against parental authority, and it did not last long.

The Young Zoologist

In Sri Lanka in those days, after students completed Grade 12 and sat for the university entrance exams, there was a waiting period of about six to eight months before the exam results were announced and when the university courses started, if you had been successful in getting into one.

I was looking for something to do during this time and came across an organization called the Young Zoologists' Association, or YZA. It was a club with an objective of furthering education on wildlife and environmental issues among youth in the country. It was run out of the Colombo Zoo by a bunch of guys and gals in high school or just after high school. They did a number of interesting things such as being active in the zoo as volunteers, helping to run the children's petting areas, and arranging for seminars, talks, and film showings related to nature and wildlife. They also had an active social set-up, with parties and road trips throughout the year.

As I had always been interested in anything related to wildlife, nature, and the environment, this looked like a pretty neat club for me to join. I became aware of YZA during a visit to the zoo with a bunch of my friends where we took a guided tour led by YZA volunteers. They seemed to be a likeable bunch of interesting boys and girls, all from Colombo schools just like us, all around our age. So, a friend and I joined the YZA. The meetings were held every Saturday afternoon at the zoo and included free admission.

I was with the YZA for about two years, part of that time as an organizing committee member. We arranged seminars and film shows and invited wildlife experts to come and give talks. We also worked sometimes at the zoo's petting area. We handled things like pythons, snakes, leopard cubs, and a host of other baby animals that had been born at the zoo and were being familiarized with humans so that they could be exhibited at the petting area for school children. I had a pretty interesting time at YZA. Its annual road trip to a far-off place in Sri Lanka was a real blast. In the two years I was with the YZA we did a road trip to Hikkaduwa Beach and a road trip to Kitulgala, deep in the southwestern rainforest, where the famous movie, The Bridge on the River Kwai, was filmed. I remember that on that trip we had a bunch of musical instruments with us and we marched along the river there playing the famous Colonel Bogey March from the movie. Unforgettable memories!

Since that time, YZA has grown. It now has a strong web presence and appears to be very active. It gives me such pleasure when I see their announcements and notices come up on the web and on social media. We were the pioneers of that organization.

So that, in a nutshell, was how my late teen years went by. It was an interesting time. I could not have asked for anything better.

The Stuff We Ate: Ambul Thyal, Pol Sambal, and Rice

Sri Lankan food is a fusion of Indian Subcontinental, Southeast Asian, Arabian, and of course colonial European cooking. The food really reflects the ethnic mix of the country. Until recently, the rest of the world had not heard of or tasted Sri Lankan food, but it is now being discovered.

The most common food combination that was cooked and served in our houses those days was of course rice and curry. Sri Lankans curry everything under the sun: fish, meat, veggies; anything edible can and will be made into a curry. This method of cooking originates from the times when there were no refrigeration facilities in homes and food had to be spiced up to the hilt to preserve it. The flavour and the taste will vary with the type of curry powders that are used in a particular dish, and there are different curry powders that you use for meat, fish, and vegetables.

The number one Sri Lankan food item that is guaranteed to evoke curiosity and puzzlement among non–Sri Lankans or anyone who has not lived in or visited the country is hoppers. I can hear you ask, "What in the devil are hoppers? Don't tell me that you guys eat grasshoppers over there?" No, we do not eat grasshoppers, at least not yet.

A hopper is a rice pancake. In local languages it is called aappa or appam. It is made out of rice flour batter, slightly fermented by adding some coconut water or a bit of yeast. It is prepared in a deep, curved wok and has crisp edges and a thick, soft centre. You can break an egg into the wok as the hopper is being made and make it into an egg hopper. You usually eat them with a fish or meat curry, dipping pieces in the curry. Why are they called hoppers? Who knows! We Sri Lankans are a strange lot sometimes. Hopper-making places, "hopper huts" as they are called, are ubiquitous in Sri Lanka; pretty much every town, or village, has at least several. Lankans eat them for breakfast and dinner.

There is a Sri Lankan saying for something that is missing an important part. They say, "that's like a restaurant without hoppers". Recently, the high-end restaurants in Colombo have started serving chocolate hoppers, strawberry hoppers, and other new mind-numbing variations. The good old hopper is going upscale.

Being an island, Sri Lanka has an amazing variety of fish and other seafood. There are a number of ways to prepare fish. You curry them (of course!), you grill them, or you fry them. Fish is available fresh or dried. Dried fish (karavala) are filets which have been salted and sun-dried to last a long time without refrigeration. When you travel on coastal roads on the island, at many places you see fish filets laid down in the sun to be dried. Pumpkin curry with pieces of dried fish in it tastes divine. Interestingly enough, Sri Lanka has no tradition of sushi or anything similar. Lobster is considered a luxury and it is mostly supplied to the tourist industry. There are many types of crab in Sri Lanka, including the big fat lagoon crabs that come from the costal lagoons north of Colombo and from Jaffna, and the smaller sea crabs. Sri Lankan crab curry is one of the hottest food items these days and is catching fire all across Asia as something not to be missed. Another favourite seafood of mine is curried squid or cuttle fish.

There is a crab story that my mother used to tell. One day when we were living in Negombo, an acquaintance dropped off a bag of crabs at our house. My mom took the bag to the kitchen and opened it to find, to her horror, that they were all still alive. Soon the crabs were running all over the kitchen and my mom and the housemaid had a time trying to catch them and stuff them back in the bag. After they were all secure the bag was sent back, as my mother would not kill them.

Of all the fish dishes, my all-time favourite is what is called ambul thyal (sour fish curry). This is yellowfin tuna or skipjack cooked in a clay cooking pot over an open fire, prepared to be a dry, dark, and sour curry using specific spices and one particular dried fruit we call goraka (brindleberry or Indian tamarind). This is a unique dish that comes from Southern Sri Lanka. Being from that area, both my grandma and my mother knew how to cook this very well. You ate ambul thyal with red rice and pol sambal, which is freshly grated coconut, red onions, chili powder, lime juice, and salt, with a sprinkle of Maldive fish powder.* The whole mix is softly ground on a flat block of granite with a granite rolling pin to make a red sambal.

This combination of rice, pol sambal, and ambul thyal was for us so unbeatable that we would eat it in any quantity, at any time. In my opinion, if you do not like pol sambal, you are not Sri Lankan. It is one of those intangible things that defines a Sri Lankan, that and a liking for Baila and being crazy about cricket. Clay cooking pots and open-fire hearths are a thing of the past in most Sri Lankan kitchens now. The ambul thyal that is cooked in aluminum pans on gas stoves really does not taste the same. Oh, the price of progress.

Talking about meats in Sri Lanka, there is the famous Sri Lankan bistake. In most hole-in-the-wall eating places, street

---

* Maldive fish is a boiled and sun-dried tuna unique to the Maldives. It's a very popular fish flavouring in Sri Lankan cooking when preparing vegetable dishes.

restaurants, and in school and office cafeterias, one always comes across thora maalu bistake or mas bistake. The first is a fish curry made out of kingfish (thora maalu), and the other is a beef or lamb curry. Both are usually served with some bread or roti or rice. For years I could not figure out what bistake meant as it was obviously not a Sinhala word. Then suddenly it dawned on me that bistake is beef steak! Somehow, Lankans turned the term "beef steak" into "bistake" and applied it to all fish and meat dishes.

Sri Lankans do not eat exotic animals such as monkeys, snakes, birds, and small rodents like guinea pigs. Unlike in some other Asian countries, we definitely do not eat our cats or dogs. They are valued pets. The meat we eat includes chicken, pork, beef, lamb, and sometimes rabbit. In the areas close to jungles, one may get wild boar and venison, although they are illegal to hunt. We also do not eat escargots (snails, to the uninitiated), nor do we eat frog legs. This is despite the island being overrun with so many varieties of frogs. The French never colonized Sri Lanka, so the frogs got a lucky break!

In the late seventies, when the economy was opened to outside investments, all of a sudden there was an influx of Asian construction companies that arrived with large numbers of their own nationals to work on various projects all over the country. In the surrounding towns and villages, locals suddenly discovered a new economic opportunity: the Asian foreigners loved to eat snakes! So, for a period, the local snake population had a difficult time as they were hunted down for profit. Fortunately, there were and still are enough snakes to go around and the "Cheenas", as the locals called the Asians, could not make any significant dent in the snake population of the country. Did you know that the late Steve Irwin called Sri Lanka the Island of Snakes? One wonders if he meant just the slithering kind or if this included the two-legged snakes which seem to populate political circles these days.

Contrary to what many outsiders think, Buddhism does not impose any restrictions on eating meat. Hindus may not eat beef, and Muslims and Jews may not eat pork; but we Buddhists can munch away on any meat to our heart's content if we want to. Vegetarianism is a choice for Buddhists and not an edict or a law. This sounds puzzling to non-believers because, as I said before, one of the main precepts in Buddhism is "thou shall not kill or take life". As for our family, in true Buddhist style, meat was consumed in moderation with fish being the main "flesh" that we ate.

When we were young, our family had no tradition of going out for a meal at a restaurant. That was a middle-class thing. One did not eat "food from the road". If we ate out, it was always at a friend's or relative's place. The only time we ate at a restaurant or a hotel was when we went on a road trip and there was no relative's or friend's house to raid for a meal.

In the sixties there were also very few restaurants where one could have food that was hygienically prepared and safe to eat. The few commercial places that my family felt comfortable with were the really high-end restaurants or hotels, which were really expensive. The only time we went to those was when we got invited to a wedding or a party. So in general, my mother was dead set against us eating out. "Don't eat that trash. It is not safe. You will fall sick," was her almost automatic response to any eating-out suggestion.

As we grew up, our aversion to street food slowly disappeared. One thing that changed was we didn't have to tell our mom each time we ate out. All my friends were happily eating out without ending up in hospital for food poisoning. Often when we went for a movie in Colombo we would go to a place like the Greenlands, Perera & Sons, or The Fab for food. These were among the few decent eat-out places in the city that we could go to without breaking our meagre wallets. The situation is entirely different now. There are many restaurants in the city, some of them even considered world-class. All of a sudden, almost without anyone noticing, Sri Lankan food has been discovered by the world and is much sought after.

To get back to the seventies food scene of us teenagers, there were a few staples that we always had outside our houses. These are the items that I used to love, and I wish we had them in Toronto. The first such food that comes to mind is the simple bun. Unlike the buns that you get in the West, they are slightly sweet and of elongated shape, like a hot dog bun but with tapered ends with some sugar sprinkled on the top. We called them kimbula banis, or "crocodile buns", because they were shaped like a crocodile. Our son subsisted on them during his first visits to the country. Those and hoppers.

Then there was the cheap lunch of students and many office workers, rose paan and parippu, which is basically half a loaf of roasted bread and a plate of lentil curry. You broke off pieces of the bread, dipped them in the gravy, and ate. This was delicious, and we used to eat it most days at our school cafeteria. Then of course the previously mentioned pol sambal, which we ate with rice, bread, or roti.

Another of our favourites was boiled sweet yams or cassava with a fiery curry of meat or fish. Roti or thosai were also great takeout food from the numerous Tamil shops in the city. Roti came in all kinds of forms and with fillings like meat, eggs, or veggies. Kottu roti, which has now taken the island by storm, is a recent invention. It is chopped-up plain roti mixed with lots of spices, veggies, eggs, and if you prefer, lamb or beef, almost like a spicy pasta or a risotto. If you do not like spices or react badly to them, you are warned not to go anywhere near a kottu roti.

When you talk about Sri Lankan food, you have to mention "short eats". These are buns with fillings and savoury pastries that are front and centre at any party, wedding reception, or other celebration. They also figured prominently on road trips and journeys that we went on when we were young. These are spicy snacks, almost always breaded and fried or baked. They could be fish buns (maalu paan), beef buns (mas paan), cutlets (beef or fish balls, breaded and deep-fried), vadai (deep-fried lentil balls), or many other varieties. Fortunately for us, most of these are now available in Toronto's many Sri Lankan restaurants.

Sri Lanka also has many mouth-watering traditional desserts, some so full of sugar and coconut oil that just looking at them would shoot your blood sugar and cholesterol levels through the roof. We also have the full gamut of Western cakes, puddings, and other desserts.

Then there are of course chutneys, pickles, and other concoctions that are endless in variations and combinations. Sri Lanka being a tropical country, the variety of fruits and vegetables that you see over there is absolutely amazing. Mango, guava, pineapple, durian, mangosteen, rambutan, star fruit, sapodilla: the list is endless, so the possibilities for chutneys and pickles are also endless. So are the possibilities for making fruit drinks.

As mentioned earlier, suddenly the world has discovered Sri Lankan cuisine. These days the tourists are flocking to Colombo and beyond for local food experiences. You can take a fancy food tour there or go to a local house and watch an aunty make a traditional Sri Lankan meal. There are boutique hotels everywhere with good chefs who will take you to the local market so that you can select the freshest of fish that they will cook for you back in the hotel while you watch.

The hottest of all Sri Lankan dishes (in every sense) these days is crab curry. I think the unique tastes of the Sri Lankan version are due to the murunga[*] leaves that we add to the

---

[*] Also known as moringa in the West.

curry. The best crab curries come from Jaffna, in the north. Some of the crab restaurants in Colombo are rated best in the world and would require the monthly salary of an average Sri Lankan worker to go and eat there. Fortunately, you do not have to go to the Ministry of Crab, one of the fanciest and most expensive restaurants in Colombo, to eat crab; instead, you can go to the local fish market, buy a bunch of crabs, take them home, and cook them yourself.

It goes without saying there was no McDonald's, no Burger King, no Pizza Hut, and no Tim Hortons at that time. We had not heard of fast food till we saw it in Western movies. Now they have made an appearance there, and I am not convinced at all that it is a good thing. However, some of the fast-food chains have acknowledged the local tastes: you can get a spicy pizza at Pizza Hut in Colombo and apparently there are seeni sambol burgers at Sri Lankan McDonald's, seeni sambol being the sweet and fiery fried onion filling that we Sri Lankans love.

Of Fishermen and Lighthouse Keepers: My Parents' Story

No story of my childhood would be complete without talking about my parents, Aluthvala Tantirige Samarapala and Sembukuttige Sriya De Silva. The simple fact is that I am who I am today because of them. They both came from the southern coast, my father from the sleepy little fishing village of Hikkaduwa and my mother from the nearby southern town of Galle.

Father's Story

The old court records show that many generations ago, during the Dutch colonial times, my ancestors came to Sri Lanka from the Indian state of Kerala on the west coast of the subcontinent. At that time many migrants came from India and settled along the southwestern coast of Ceylen or Ceylon, which is what Sri Lanka was called in those days. The records show that my direct ancestors, fishing folk, settled in the area just north of Galle where the small towns of Ambalangoda and Hikkaduwa are today. In fact, both my last name, Tantirige, and my mother's maiden name, Sembukuttige, are derived from Malayalam, the principle language of Kerala. Over the years, lots of Indians have asked me if I am from Kerala. I have been told that "Tantirige" in Malayalam means the house of musicians or people who specialized in tantric music. Very much in line with my own interest in music!

My ancestors would have been Catholic then, as a lot of Keralites still are. Somewhere along the way, their descendants converted to Buddhism and moved from being fishermen to being local businessmen who supplied the fishing villages in the area. Most of this story was unearthed by my father, who searched through old Dutch court records in the Galle courts detailing land transactions. He was planning to get translated copies of these records, but didn't manage to before he passed away in 1999.

In 2009, at my nephew's wedding reception, I was talking to one of my relatives explaining our family history and the connection to Kerala and our name to music.

The band is playing, and suddenly we hear a familiar voice singing. We look up to see my sister up on the stage, merrily singing with the band! The guy I was talking to looks at me and says, "OK, you don't have to convince me. You people are from a house of music." Instant validation!

My father was a remarkable man. He was from a large family with three brothers and five sisters. They were a prominent business family in Hikkaduwa and they owned significant amounts of land there. They lived in an old mansion with a large garden. Although wealthy by the village's standards, the children, especially the boys, had duties and obligations to the family that they were expected to fulfill. My grandfather's business was trading. He would get all kinds of goods from Colombo and distribute them to local traders, and bought local produce like rice, coconuts, and cinnamon and dispatched them to the big trading houses in Colombo. He was a local middleman. When my father was around ten years old, his job was to receive the goods from the Colombo train, load them onto carts, and make sure that they were distributed on time to the local traders. These duties were in addition to going to school.

My grandparents in the 1930s were very well aware of the value and opportunities of a good formal education and were determined that the three boys would get that. My father's sisters were also educated up to higher grades, but it was expected that, when the time came, they would stop school and get married. This was a time when women were not allowed to work, although two of my aunts still managed to become teachers. The three boys in the family went on to do really well after completing their education. The eldest became a high-level officer in the civil service and the youngest became a doctor. My father entered the education service as a teacher after university and retired as a Director of Education, managing large numbers of schools in various parts of the island.

When I think of my father's life story I am in awe and at the same time a bit envious. What a life he had. Here was a boy born and brought up in a small, nondescript village in a far-off corner of Sri Lanka. He got an excellent education, starting at the village temple, then at the village school, followed by the high school in a nearby town. He was in the first or second batch to enter the then newly minted University of Ceylon. They were an extraordinary bunch of students; many went on to become politicians and civil servants that ran the country after independence. My father was in university during World War II when the island had massive British and Allied bases. After the war he saw the country gain independence from the British. In fact, he assisted his professor in preparing some of the commemorative documentation that were issued on the day of the independence. After he completed his BA, he entered the Education Service as a teacher and then entered the education administration, gradually rising in the hierarchy and retiring as a Director of Education.

He was an excellent photographer who set up and ran the photography club at St. Anthony's College in Kandy, the first school where he served as a teacher. He was a Boy Scout officer and, for a brief time in the late seventies, was the Assistant Commissioner of Scouts for the Sri Lanka Scout Association. He participated in scouting jamborees and led Scout delegations to nearby countries. He travelled outside the country many times and was in Toronto just before he passed away suddenly when he was seventy-two years old.

On top of all that, he could play the flute, knew some steps in Sri Lankan traditional dancing, and was a very good artist and an excellent photographer. One of our cherished possessions is a pencil sketch portrait of our son Sanjay that he did while in Toronto. It still hangs in our living room. He completed this sketch just a few weeks before he passed away.

He was a self-taught mechanic who could dismantle and reassemble his car (with the help of my cousins and me). He would think nothing of dismantling our radio when it did not work, even though he had no formal science education or technical training in his life. Sometimes he would be up to his eyeballs in an impossible attempt of maintenance or repair of one of our household electrical items and I would say to him, "Fools rush in where angels fear to tread." He would look the other way, not wanting to let me see that he was smiling. He never hesitated if there was a chance to help anyone. There are many people today beyond just my sister and me who owe the current state of their lives to my father because he helped them and directed them to the right career.

While doing all of this he also raised a family as the sole breadwinner, built a house and paid it off completely, raised two kids, one who earned an MSc in chemistry in Russia and became a senior manager at a prominent cosmetics company in Sri Lanka, and one who ended up in Canada with three degrees in engineering. Not bad for a native boy born in a small village at a small corner of a simple, unimportant third world country in the early years of the twentieth century. A life well lived and experienced indeed.

He was straight as an arrow and honest to a fault. In the early 1960s the government of the day decided to take over and run most of the schools in the country. They had been previously run by various religious organizations such as the Catholic Church, the Anglican Church, and other such non-governmental organizations. The takeover of the schools was based on an arbitration process that figured out the amount of compensation that had to be awarded to various organizations who were losing their schools. It was a complex process that had to value all the physical structures, such as buildings and equipment, that were being taken over by the government.

My father was on the team that represented the government during this arbitration process. It has been said that if he was not honest, he could have made a fortune by shaping the arbitration decisions one way or the other. Apparently there were ample chances to do so, but he could not be bought. Later one of his friends made a remark to me that if anyone had questions about my father's honesty, they just had to look at the house we lived in, the car we drove, and the lifestyle we maintained. That would be enough for anyone to know that my dad did not take a cent through any dishonest means from anyone. This has stayed with me throughout my life, and every time I have had to make some moral decision or a judgment, my first thought is, *What would Dad do?* You set a high standard to live up to, Dad.

He was fearless when he knew he was right and stubborn as a mule when people tried to direct him in a way he did not want to go. In Sri Lanka, when a government changes following an election, the incoming government will "clean house". The people that the incoming administration think are not their supporters are removed from important government departments and ministries. Those whose loyalty to the new administration is suspect and who work in Colombo offices are sent on what were called "punishment transfers" to far-off outstation areas. My father was sent on such transfers several times in his career. What most people did not realize was he did not mind these transfers because they gave him the opportunity to travel to far-flung corners of the island.

I remember that when the government changed in 1977 he was sent to Anuradhapura education district, which is considered a difficult area to serve. Away from Colombo, it used to be mostly jungle with a few small towns and agricultural land surrounding tiny villages. At that time, some of the schools in the remote villages could only be reached by walking many miles through jungle on footpaths where wild elephants and other animals roamed, as there were no drivable roads to these villages. There was risk of malaria. Within a few months of his arrival in this area, my father had visited every single school in his new district, some of which he found in a state of absolute decay. People in those villages told my father that it was the first time they had seen an education officer visiting these schools in many years, and some places had never been visited even once.

My father also had strong views on our religion and how you should follow it. He was Buddhist through and through, but he did not believe that you had to be forced to participate in religion just because you are Buddhist. I never ever saw him going to a temple to worship or pray. Often, he would drop by the local temple and would chat away with his priest friends — but worship with them and pray at a shrine room or by a stupa? I never saw him do that. He was attuned to the buzz on local politics and what was happening in the country: he knew that the best place to hear local political gossip was at the temple or the church.

One incident that happened in his late life illustrates what he thought of organized religion. In our neighbourhood in Mount Lavinia, there were several large weaving mills making clothing material. One time, one of these mills was having a week-long Buddhist event. Every evening Buddhist priests were brought to the factory and there would be a service and chanting that went on for a couple of hours. To show that they were good citizens of the area, they would broadcast these services and chanting over a sound system that could be heard all over the neighbourhood. My father, living just a short distance away, was incensed. He wanted peace and quiet at home and resented the fact that he was being forced to listen to loud Buddhist chanting that went on for hours on end. In his mind, no one should be forced to listen to anything that he or she did not want to hear.

He protested, but to no avail. So off he goes to the local temple where he thought the priests came from and tells the head priest, "Sir, with these monks shouting like cattle, a man cannot even sleep in peace." However, the offending priests were not from the local temple. So, the head priest, who happened to be his friend, replied, "Please sir, they are not my cattle." We heard this story when the same head priest visited our house for last rites on my father's passing. He told us, "Your dad never hesitated to say what was on his mind, even when he was talking to a priest."

Mother's Story

So much for my father. Who is Sriya de Silva Sembukuttige? At the time of writing she is still alive, living in Sri Lanka with my sister, ninety years of age and in bad health, her mind and memories completely jumbled and mixed due to dementia and Alzheimer's. She cannot move on her own, so she sits all day, hardly recognizing the people around her, talking about imaginary situations and imaginary times. It is a devastating condition that is tough on her and her children.

She was born in the town of Galle, in southern Sri Lanka. She had one brother who was a doctor. She was educated to a high level of education at the Galle Convent run by Catholic nuns. Her father worked for the British Navy in the Imperial Lighthouse Service in the first half of the twentieth century, including during both world wars. As a part of his service he was stationed in lighthouses all over the Indian Ocean, Sri Lanka, the Maldives Islands, and on most of the small islands in the Northern Indian Ocean where the Brits had lighthouses.

My mother spent part of her life at the southernmost point in Sri Lanka, at Dondra Head (Devinuwara), where one of the tallest lighthouses in Asia is located. Their house, which was the lighthouse keeper's residence, was right on the beach next to the lighthouse. It is an amazing place, beautiful and wild. If you head straight south from Dondra Head, you will not see any land until you hit the land mass and icefields of Antarctica more than 10,000 kilometres away. In every sense, this is the edge of the Asian continent. We have been to this lighthouse a few times on our trips down south, and I was fortunate to take our son there in 2013 to show him where *Archchi* grew up all those years ago. I still cannot believe that someone could be so fortunate as to live in a place like that. These days people pay hundreds of dollars for a week's stay in similar locales.

My mother has told me many stories about that place, of the blue whales that spout offshore, and of giant turtles that come ashore at night and crawl straight inside the house because that is exactly the place where they would have come to lay eggs on that beach before there was a house. She has talked of big sharks that would come to the bay next to the house because people those days dumped household waste there. She remembers reading a book or studying on the beach, seated on the rocks while watching flying fish skim over the water in the bay. She has talked of fishermen pulling huge fishing nets ashore in the bay, and of their chants. She was not allowed anywhere close to the nets as they were pulled in. It was a hard job pulling them to the shore and so there was lots of cussing among the fishermen as they pulled. What she learned there she applied to us when we were young and at a beach, forbidding us to go anywhere near where a fishing net was being pulled in.

It was an absolutely magical place to grow up, the sort of setting that you usually only read about. When we were young, my sister and I never could understand in our simple minds why she moved away from this place and why we were not living in a spot like that. I remember secretly wishing that my father was a lighthouse keeper. My parent's wedding was held there, in the garden of the lighthouse. Their formal wedding photo has the stone house in which my mother lived as the backdrop. There are photos that my father took from his own camera that day from the top of the lighthouse. How did he find time to go up there and take photos on his wedding day?

Once my mother completed the General Certificate of Education (GCE), she was withdrawn from school. By this time, she was fluent in reading, writing, and conversing in English, a huge achievement for a local girl at that time (the late 1940s) in Sri Lanka. She was offered a position at her school to teach English, but her father did not agree to her going to work. Women from "good" families did not work — that is how the thinking went in those days. What a waste. Women could vote in elections — universal suffrage had been in place in Sri Lanka since 1931 — but they could not work.

My mother could have been a good teacher as she had a knack for explaining things and did not get emotionally worked up easily. When we ask her why she did not demand that she be allowed to work, she sighs and says very gently that it was how things were in those days. I am sure she would have loved to work, and although she never made a great fuss about it, she must regret that she was not allowed to. She did not want to go against her parents' wishes. When the time came for my sister to leave home, and the country, to go to Russia for five years, my mother, who had been strict during my sister's upbringing, did not object. She must have thought about opportunities that had been denied to her and decided that she would not stand in the way of her daughter.

So, what did an educated young woman do after leaving school? Usually they were married off quickly, with the family finding a suitable man. How did you find a suitable man? That is where family connections and matchmakers came into play. What criteria did they use to make a match? Religion and caste were absolutely important; then came the family's status, their wealth, and the man's job. A guy with a government job would be a good catch as that gave status, money, and security. There was no question of finding anyone on your own. For one, you would not have much opportunity to meet men of your age, and even if you did have the chance to meet someone, you were not supposed to fall in love. That is what "loose girls" did. You had to wait until your parents found your man. Marry first and then fall in love, that was the expectation and the rule.

While my mother was waiting to get married, her mother taught her things like cooking, sewing, embroidery — things that a good newly married woman had to know! I do not know how my mother and father were "arranged". Which family approached which and who led the negotiations is not known to us. Anyway, everything must have fallen into place, stars aligned, horoscopes were scrutinized and found to be matching, the details of the two families looked into and found to be agreeable to both sides with no hidden scandals. Interestingly enough, they did not get married right away after the two families made the connection. The wedding took place a couple of years after they had been introduced to each other, which was rather unusual for that time. We do not know why. But this gave the young couple a chance to get to know each other before they got married. Nearly fifty years after their marriage, when I was sorting through my father's papers after he passed away, I came across letters that they had exchanged at that time. They are cute to read: nothing steamy or heavy, just showing affection to each other, my mother complaining that he did not come to visit her as much as she wanted him to.

They got married in 1951. My sister was born in 1952 and I followed in 1955. By all accounts they had a fantastic life together, looking after each other lovingly. I never saw them shouting or yelling at each other; I am sure there were times when they had disagreements, but nothing lasted and nothing major happened. From the number of stories that we heard from them about the early years of their life together, it is certain that they had a good time. We have heard repeatedly of the places they lived, the things they did, the friends they had. You got the feeling that it was a harmonious life.

My mother seemed to be a person who was happy with what she had and what she had been given in life. I remember that after many years of marriage, my mother still would wait in the late afternoon for my father to come home from work. She would be seated in the veranda of our house, and when he arrived home she would bring him a cup of tea and they would sit there chatting happily away, talking about anything and everything. Only after they'd had some time together would she get up and start preparing the evening dinner. Sometimes when they were yapping away, we kids would say to each other that the two lovebirds were chirping!

Mother was a good cook and loved to bake. She collected recipes and on weekends always made something special for us. She had a scrapbook of recipes that she had collected from various magazines that were available at that time. She could make all kinds of cakes and puddings. She was also a good seamstress and made all my sister's dresses. She did beautiful embroidery. Most of the cushion covers and the bed covers at our home were sewn by her with stunning embroidered patterns. All the curtains at our house were made by her. Once when I was in Grade 8, she and I made a large carpet for our living room as a part of a school project. I remember that she was so proud of this, pointing out to visitors that she and I had done it.

She absolutely loved the cats and the dog we had in our home. We used to tease her that she cared more for her pet dog than her children. She was also in charge of flowers in our garden. Father looked after the fruit trees and Mom looked after the flowerbeds and vegetable patches. In gardening, I was always her handyman and general labourer. I dug all the flowerbeds and helped her to plant.

My mother had one or two quirky habits. Every day our household received a couple of newspapers, one in Sinhala and one in English. She would read these from cover to cover: news, opinion, features, comics, obituaries, and even the advertisements. But she did not read books, which was rather unusual in a house full of books. We tried our best to get her interested in reading them but were not successful. She also loved the Sri Lankan soap operas, first on the radio and later on TV after it was introduced in the country in the late seventies. She would not miss a single episode. She also did not sing. I have never ever heard her singing except the lullabies that she sang to me when I was very little. This was unusual at our house, which was always full of music. There was always someone singing something, me or my sister or one of our cousins. If we were not singing, the radio or a cassette player would be almost always on, playing a tune. But my mother never sang. Strange indeed.

Our mom was also the keeper of religion in our family. As in most Sri Lankan households, we had a place where we maintained a modest shrine with a small statue of Buddha and other Buddhist paraphernalia. My mother ensured that from every meal we had in our house, a tiny portion would be placed in front of Buddha in the shrine room as an offering. This is the Buddhist way of saying grace. As the sun went down every evening, before the house lights were turned on, she would light a tiny oil lamp in a small alcove that had been built on one of the boundary walls. Every evening, before dinner, Mom would also say a few Buddhist prayers at the shrine after placing there a few flowers plucked from the garden. As she got older the prayer time got longer and longer, and on the full moon day of every month she would spend the whole day at the temple taking part in various religious ceremonies and rituals. Most of these were normal activities that took place in every Buddhist household in Sri Lanka.

Although my father was the breadwinner of the family, my mother was the overall authority and decision maker. She had the final say on how and on what the money was spent. She decided what we ate, what we wore, and where we went. In short, most of the important decisions about the family were taken by her. My father just went along, bringing in the money. This was not unusual in Sri Lanka at that time. Men earned the money and women decided how it was spent. One time I remember a friend of mine explaining very politically incorrectly how this set-up operated. He said, "We men have the difficult tasks. We have to solve world hunger, settle Middle East peace problems, and end the Cold War. Our women, they have the easy tasks. All they have do is to decide how the family money is spent, where we go for vacations, what colour the curtains will be, and what to buy at the market that day." I don't think he would dare to say it like that these days. Women have much more say in matters outside the home and the family now, but there is a long way to go before the society can be seen as giving equal opportunity to both sexes.

Our mom and dad had two different personalities. Father was outgoing, intellectual, curious about the world he lived in, and made friends everywhere he went. Mother was shy, kept to herself, and was only comfortable within her own extended family and her limited circle of friends. She was set in her ways and thinking. She was not used to being teased, and we only realized much later that she had lots of insecurities.

There is a photograph of them taken in 1951. They are coming back home to my father's childhood home after their honeymoon. They are posing at the entrance to the courtyard of the house in Hikkaduwa. She is nicely dressed in a beautiful sari holding a bouquet of flowers and my father is in a nice suit. We were very familiar with this photo and we used to call it Mom and Dad's homecoming photo. Now when I look at this photo, I see fear in her eyes. She looks terrified! She was from a small family, just her older brother and her. They were a middle-class family of modest means. Now she had married this guy and was joining his comparatively well-to-do, large family with five teen girls (none of them married at that time) and three boys who lived in a mansion of a house in Hikkaduwa. No wonder she looks so intimidated.

My mother was never very comfortable with my father's family. Although they have always been kind to us, she always had some reservations about them. My sister and I would simply laugh at her about this. We know that my father's family never, ever, treated my mother badly. Over the years, my sister and I have talked about this a lot because we simply cannot understand why our mother had such feelings. The conclusion that we came to was that she had a sheltered upbringing. She was educated in a convent by Catholic nuns, and she really was not encouraged to interact with common people. This left her with lots of insecurities and fears about the world just outside her comfort circle. Joining this large, relatively wealthy, outgoing family in marriage, she must have felt like a fish out of water. So much for armchair psychoanalysis.

One thing that I still remember with gratitude is that there was absolutely no corporal punishment in our house. This was unusual in a society where parents regarded physical punishment of their children as their right and duty. My friends got regular beatings for all kinds of issues. It could be for bad behaviour, a bad report card, breaking family rules, breaking cutlery, not eating, eating too much; it was an endless list. There was none of that in our house. In fact, my father never ever raised his voice in anger. However, if he was upset or angry, boy did we know it. My mother on the other hand was always vocal in her opinions about us, and was especially hard on my sister. I think I always received more favourable treatment than my sister from her. The strange thing about all that was even if we knew that there were no harsh discipline measures, we knew that our parents' word was law. If we wanted to do something and they said no, it was a no. I can only be thankful for them not abusing that power that they held over us.

Many times over the years when I was at an impasse with our son and didn't know what to do, I would in my mind ask my late father "Dad, how did you make this kid-raising business look so easy? You tricked me into thinking that all this was going to be a piece of cake!" I am sure he must be looking on from someplace, chuckling gently to himself.

More Than Just Six Fingers: My Sister

I think it is time to introduce my sister Mala more formally. She has already appeared at many places in this narrative. Needless to say, she played an important part in my early life, and I consider this story as her story also.

Three years older than me, she was my leader in many ways while we were growing up. When I look back at those days, it seems that I simply followed whatever she did. I started reading because she was reading. She is musically minded, and I followed her into music. She entered university to do a science degree, and I followed her to engineering. I was a shy kid in my preteen years and always wanted to have my sister's ability to relate to other people. I would watch her interacting with people and wish that I knew how to be that way.

She has one physical feature that makes her stand out from pretty much everyone else. She has six fingers on her left hand. Yes, six fingers. Her thumb has a smaller one attached to it. The story is that when she was born, no one noticed it the first few weeks as she was making a tight fist, hiding the extra digit. Then they discovered that she had an extra thumb. The doctors had advised my parents that while it could be removed surgically, there could be a slight risk to her main thumb during the surgery. So, my parents decided to leave it as it is. I don't think it affected her in any way. A standard joke in our family circle was that she could never have career in crime as the police would be onto her quickly using fingerprints. How many six-fingered criminals do you have around?

When Sanjay met his aunt for the first time — this was when he was about six or seven years old — he got a real shock when he saw her sixth finger. I remember he was so scared he ran into his room! Then, once he understood what it is and how it came to be, he wanted to take her to his school for show and tell.

In 1970, when she was eighteen years old, my sister went to study in Moscow. To me that was a momentous decision that she took, and it is even more remarkable that our parents, especially our mother, agreed to it. It was when I watched her boarding the flight to Russia that it became clear to me that I wanted to go abroad one day as well.

I think it really opened my eyes to the possibilities that I had in this world. Up to that point I really had not thought about my future, what I wanted to do in life and how I would do it. For the first time in my life I also felt the loneliness of someone's absence and the loss of an important support pillar in my life that had been there for me, and one that I had taken for granted. I think in an inexplicable way, her actions changed the direction of my life path also.

She returned from Moscow with an MSc in Chemistry in 1975. After she came back she taught at a high school in a town close to Mount Lavinia and then went to work in the private sector as a manager responsible for quality control and product development at a cosmetics and toiletries facility in Colombo. She left the workforce after the birth of her second child, electing to support her husband's growing businesses in gemstones while taking care of the children. I have always wondered if that was the right decision. Her two children are now grown up and are living in Australia.

Mala Akka (as I always called her; "akka", as I said before, means big sister) has a lively personality. She makes friends easily, treats everyone the same way, and is not afraid to state her opinion on anything under the sun. I still remember when she was around fifteen years old, her arguing politics with her aunts. She would not give an inch and went head to head with the aunts that were many years older than her. We all thought that she would be a lawyer one day. In a way, she resembles our father very much.

During our early years at Gothami Mavatha she was a natural leader among the neighbourhood kids. She was of course one of the main organizers of the neighbourhood concerts I mentioned. She was also the unofficial neighbourhood librarian of the children in the area, keeping track of who had which book. This was important as we could not afford to buy many books, so had to know who had borrowed what. These days she is also the one that keeps in contact with almost all of our extended family, which is spread all over the world. This is convenient for me, because I just have to talk to her to find out how everyone is doing!

She introduced me to Western pop music. This was in the midsixties, and Elvis was the King. My sister and her girlfriends were absolutely crazy about him. They had scrapbooks full of his photos, cut out from newspapers and magazines, with the lyrics of his songs lovingly copied down in cursive writing. There was a story in those days that the girls were talking about Elvis so much that one of their younger siblings went to their mom and told her, "Mom, they are always talking about a boy named Elvis, you have to do something about it!"

Back then there was a small, inexpensive magazine of about ten pages that was issued monthly in Colombo. It was called The Popular Favourites and it contained lyrics to the popular Western pop music of the time and a full-page photo of a singer. I remember my sister had to have this every month and would pester our parents till they bought it for her. Then she and her girlfriends would studiously learn the songs till they knew the lyrics by heart.

She is a great singer and ready to burst into song any time. When she was studying in Moscow, the Sri Lankan students there had a band that was popular at the university. She sang lead in that band, and sang with the band at her son's wedding reception. She is the first to be on the dance floor at any party. She has an encyclopedia of knowledge on Sinhala music and movies. If you wanted to know the latest gossip about the Sinhalese TV and movie personalities, she was the one that you spoke to. She would not miss a single episode of the countless Sri Lankan TV soap operas that are on every week. She is a voracious reader, just like me. One big difference between her and me is she is not interested in sports, while I am the opposite.

Over time she has developed an amazing talent for handicraft, quilting, and cross-stitching. She has given our whole family many mementoes of her work. Her work has been shown in exhibitions and has won awards. She has been interviewed on TV for her handicraft creations. She is the celebrity in our family. Since her kids left the country, she has been taking music lessons on electronic keyboard.

She is also one of the kindest and most down-to-earth people that I know. We have an unbreakable bond between the two of us. In the last few years she has had a tough time looking after our mother who is in bad health. I feel that she has done more than her share and has even taken on my share. It amazes me that she has not lost her sense of humour and has not lost who she is. She is a case study in grace under very trying conditions. I am so fortunate to have her as my sister.

The Sun Never Sets

As a part of a large extended family, we have many cousins. Just counting my first cousins, from the brothers and sisters of my mom and dad, we have twenty-two. Then if we count the children of my mom's and dad's cousins, the number gets close to a hundred! Obviously we were not close with each and every one of them, but we were in close contact with our twenty-two first cousins when we were growing up. We met most of them at least a few times every year, at weddings, funerals, birthday parties, or family religious events. As happens in any large group, especially when you are blood relatives, there were always conflicts, disputes, allegiances. It was exhausting just trying to figure out how everyone was getting on with each other as you had to be careful with invitations when you were planning events.

Out of these cousins, the three boys from my mother's brother, Asoka, Vasantha, and Chan, were the closest to me and my sister. The unspoken rule in our family circle was that no matter what, the five of us would always be together. The five, with their respective families, are now spread throughout the world. I am in Canada, Vasantha is in the United States, Chan lives in Australia, and my sister and Asoka are in Sri Lanka. Getting together is now somewhat difficult, but we try.

When the story of my life in these times are told, the influence of Asoka and Vasantha, the two cousins that are closest to me in age, personalities, and even in physical stature, looms large over me. These two were my brothers and friends. The third boy of that set, Chan, was a few years younger to us so he was more of a little brother than a friend. He had his own circle of friends in the neighbourhood. Asoka, Vasantha, and I hung out with the same guys. We did a lot of things together, including dismantling and repairing our car. More about that later.

After completing high school, Asoka did not go on to further studies. He trained in the highly skilled trade of diamond faceting and polishing and is one of the most skilled diamond cutters around. He was the first of us to get a job after finishing school. When he started at Blue Diamond Company in Negombo as a diamond cutter, he bought all of us leather belts from his first salary. I still have mine. It must be more than 40 years ago when I got it. Some things are worth more than their weight in diamonds.

Vasantha is a born mechanic. He can fix almost anything mechanical. After high school he joined the local flying school as an apprentice trainee, learning aircraft maintenance engineering. In those days they had one serviceable and flyable trainee aircraft and at times he would ride with the trainee pilots as they did their flying training. The flying school was close to our neighbourhood at the major airport in Colombo, and once in a while he would fly over our house on one of the trainee flights and wave to us from the aircraft.

It was no surprise to me that after a few turns in his career he ended up in Dubai working as an engineer at Emirates airline. He is now a senior engineer with them, servicing and maintaining their big jets, and at present is stationed in New York City. Chan is also an aircraft maintenance engineer. He lives and works in Australia.

Because Asoka, Vasantha, and I were the same size, we could easily exchange clothes between the three of us. I did borrow theirs more than they did mine. I suppose they did not think too much of my dress and style sense! They certainly were more fashion-conscious than I ever was. If one of us did not have a shirt to match a pair of pants for a party, no problem, one of us was sure to have something.

I can remember on evenings when we had time on our hands, especially when our parents were out, the three of us would put on a music cassette or a record of a famous Bollywood movie and dance to the tunes. Asoka was a massive Rajesh Khanna fan. He tried to comb his hair the way the actor did. He would try to copy RK's moves and we would remark behind his back, "Look at that, he looks like Rajesh Khanna with a bad case of constipation." We teased each other a lot, and still do. It is all without malice, just trash talk among very close people.

Then we have all the cousins from my father's side. We are still very close to them also. I have countless memories of our interactions with them as we were growing up. There was a time when my father's older brother lived in the heart of Colombo. As he was a senior civil servant in the government, they lived in a colonial government house with a garden full of fruit trees, on Skelton Road in Wellawatta. We used to go there frequently, oftentimes after a movie at the nearby Savoy Cinema. The third child in that set, Seneka, is just a year older than me and we could have been identical twins. We looked so similar that there were times people would mistake one of us for the other.

I remember an incident when I was about eighteen years old. I was seated in our car reading a book while my parents were shopping at the market. Suddenly, someone reaches into the car, grabs my book, and runs away with it. I am so startled as I have never seen this person in my life. He runs a few metres from the car and turns back. Then he stops and looks, and a puzzled expression comes to his face. He comes back to the car and looks at me carefully and says, "Oh my god, you are not Seneka, I am so sorry!" We had a good laugh about that.

Another set of our cousins, the five kids of my father's younger brother, lived in Moratuwa, the town next to Mount Lavinia. They used to have really nice birthday parties that we looked forward to very much. The three girls from that set and my sister got on famously and riotously. You never knew what would happen when they got together. In our family circles, these four were legendary for their antics and were known as the "crazy girls" or "pissu kello". The house this family lived in, an old mansion with hundred-year-old antique furniture, has now been turned over to a well-regarded restaurant called "Steam Boat" in Moratuwa.

Our extended family is now distributed in Canada, the United Kingdom, the United States, Sri Lanka, Australia, and New Zealand, and those are just the ones that I am aware of. One could say that the sun never sets on our extended family these days, just like the old British Empire! I don't think all of us will ever get together in one grand reunion. One of the biggest regrets that I have about living in Canada is that our son never had such an extended family environment to experience.

The Years of Living Dangerously: Communal Tensions

In the midseventies, the tensions between the Sinhalese majority and the Tamil minority of the country were slowly coming to a boil. My father, who was then the Director of Education in Homagama Educational Area, which is close to Colombo, did his part to protect the Tamil schools within his district. We were not even aware of what he was doing behind the scenes until we were invited to a farewell lunch given in his honour at Ratmalana Hindu College, a very prominent Tamil school that was under his oversight. The occasion was that he had just been transferred to a different district, one of the "punishment transfers" that occurred after the change of government in 1977. There were many prominent Tamil personalities present at this lunch, people like Somasundaram Nadesan, QC, and many others. During the speeches after the lunch, they were talking about what my father had done behind the scenes and thanked him for his efforts in bringing down tension. We as the family were astounded as he had not mentioned a word about any of this. Unfortunately, none of it mattered in the overall scheme of things as communal tensions gradually rose and Sri Lanka descended into a thirty-year war in the early eighties. However, I am glad that my father did not stand around waving his hands in despair like many did those days. In a small way, he tried to do the right thing. I am proud of him.

back to the car and looks at me carefully and says, "Oh my god, you are not Seneka, I am so sorry!" We had a good laugh about that.

Another set of our cousins, the five kids of my father's younger brother, lived in Moratuwa, the town next to Mount Lavinia. They used to have really nice birthday parties that we looked forward to very much. The three girls from that set and my sister got on famously and riotously. You never knew what would happen when they got together. In our family circles, these four were legendary for their antics and were known as the "crazy girls" or "pissu kello". The house this family lived in, an old mansion with hundred-year-old antique furniture, has now been turned over to a well-regarded restaurant called "Steam Boat" in Moratuwa.

Our extended family is now distributed in Canada, the United Kingdom, the United States, Sri Lanka, Australia, and New Zealand, and those are just the ones that I am aware of. One could say that the sun never sets on our extended family these days, just like the old British Empire! I don't think all of us will ever get together in one grand reunion. One of the biggest regrets that I have about living in Canada is that our son never had such an extended family environment to experience.

The Years of Living Dangerously: Communal Tensions

In the midseventies, the tensions between the Sinhalese majority and the Tamil minority of the country were slowly coming to a boil. My father, who was then the Director of Education in Homagama Educational Area, which is close to Colombo, did his part to protect the Tamil schools within his district. We were not even aware of what he was doing behind the scenes until we were invited to a farewell lunch given in his honour at Ratmalana Hindu College, a very prominent Tamil school that was under his oversight. The occasion was that he had just been transferred to a different district, one of the "punishment transfers" that occurred after the change of government in 1977. There were many prominent Tamil personalities present at this lunch, people like Somasundaram Nadesan, QC, and many others. During the speeches after the lunch, they were talking about what my father had done behind the scenes and thanked him for his efforts in bringing down tension. We as the family were astounded as he had not mentioned a word about any of this. Unfortunately, none of it mattered in the overall scheme of things as communal tensions gradually rose and Sri Lanka descended into a thirty-year war in the early eighties. However, I am glad that my father did not stand around waving his hands in despair like many did those days. In a small way, he tried to do the right thing. I am proud of him.

Talking about Sinhalese–Tamil tensions, my father knew some of the prominent Tamil politicians in the sixties and seventies. Most of them were his batchmates[*] at the University of Ceylon, and some of them were with him at the Union Hostel, the university student residence in Colombo. One of them was Appapillai Amirthalingam, who later became the leader of the Tamil United Liberated Front, the main Tamil opposition to the Sinhalese-led governments in the seventies. Sometimes on the weekends, a group of students would take the train from Colombo to Hikkaduwa. They would spend the morning on the beach and then have lunch at my father's house and take the evening train back to Colombo. My father remembered one such trip very well. He recalled Mr. Amirthalingam in their kitchen, seated side by side with my grandmother, both of them chatting away like two old friends as she cooked some delicious Southern Sri Lankan food for the visitors over a wood fire. He related this story to us one day and remarked, "That is how we were those days. Now the same people are trying to kill each other."

When Sri Lanka descended into war in the eighties it must have shaken my father to the core. Unlike most Sinhalese, he had many Tamil friends, coworkers, and associates. He had travelled all over the north as part of the school takeover activities and had stayed at many Tamil households as their guests. He knew them more closely than most Sinhalese did.

In 1981 there was an incident that is considered a key milestone of the conflict. On the night of June 1, a mob organized by the government went on a rampage in Jaffna, burning the library to ground. Within it were priceless Tamil documents that had been collected over centuries, many of

---

[*] Graduates of the same year.

them one of a kind and irreplaceable. It was an incalculable loss to the Tamil community and to the country. I was already in Canada by this time. I remember receiving a letter from my father about this. In it he raged about "how a bunch of ignorant idiots had destroyed a priceless collection of culture and knowledge". He raged at a government that had gone completely irrational and was hell-bent on exacting revenge for the heating-up Tamil militancy. He warned in that letter that "we as Sinhalese and as a country will pay dearly for this". Sure enough, by 1983 the country was in a war that would continue for the next thirty years.

In July 1983, following an ambush of an army patrol in the north by Tamil guerrillas, the Sinhalese mobs ran riot, murdering innocent Tamil people, burning their houses and looting their businesses. There was a lot of that in our neighbourhood in Mount Lavinia, which had a number of Tamil homes. The mobs came from outside while the area residents tried whatever they could to protect the victims, at times hiding them in their houses while the mobs looted and burned the Tamil-owned properties.

I was in Toronto when these events happened, so most of this part of the story is second-hand; I heard of all this later from my sister and my friends who were there at the time. My father and the other residents of the area had done whatever they could to protect the victims. But often it was too late. Houses were burnt and people were killed in what was clearly a premeditated and organized pogrom by the government on the Tamil population. My sister recalls driving our father to a Tamil house that had been looted and burnt. It was the residence of a friend of his. Fortunately, they had been evacuated before the mob came. My sister said that my father cried as he wandered desolately among the ruins of the burnt house. My father, the stoic man who seldom displayed any emotion, cried.

My father's Tamil friends held him in such high esteem that on his passing in 1999 one of them, Mr. Jeganathan, who was the former principal of the prominent Tamil college in Colombo called Hindu College, wrote his obituary for the national newspaper The Daily News.

This is not the story of the Sinhalese–Tamil conflict. That has been sliced, diced, and analyzed in hundreds of books, articles, films, and other media. I am just writing these stories to remember the incidents that happened years ago and hopefully through these, shine a light on the remarkable man that was my father.

Me and Harry Potter's Flying Car

How many people can claim that they have driven the flying car in the Harry Potter movies? Well, I can. We had a Ford Anglia 105E, mid-1960s vintage. It was identical to the car that appeared in the Harry Potter movies, right down to the light blue colour. My father got it in Australia where he spent a year in the midsixties on a study placement at the University of Sydney.

My father had this car for more than thirty years. I learned to drive in that car. In fact, a lot of people in my family used it to learn to drive. My sister, my brother-in-law, my nephew — they all did. It was a nice little beast of a car, practically indestructible, very powerful for its class and time. Its most prominent characteristic was the backward-slanted rear window.

I started driving before I was eligible to get a driver's licence. At that time my father was working away from Colombo, one of those times when he was on a "punishment transfer". He came home only during the weekends, so the car was sitting in our garage most of the time. So the situation was that there were three teenage boys with a car in the garage, all fuelled up and ready to go, with the owner away most of the time. What would one expect to happen? We started cautiously. Initially we would start the car in the garage and move it forward and reverse trying to understand and get a feel for the operation of the clutch. Then after a few tries we moved the car out of the garage into our driveway, and from there onto the street where we would drive it from one end to the other. I am sure that by this time the local grapevine was in full swing and my father would have heard that we were playing with his car. He did not say a thing to us.

By the time Father decided that it was time I learned to drive, I was already proficient at it. I was still below the driving age, which I think was eighteen at that time. I remember that I passed the driving test as soon as I reached the correct age. I drove that car all over Sri Lanka, from the jam-packed roads in Colombo to narrow, winding, mountain roads with 180-degree switchbacks.

Driving in Sri Lanka was hard then and is almost impossible now. You had to share two-lane roads on which you overtook a vehicle in front by driving on the lane for oncoming traffic. No passing lanes there! At that time there were no limited-access expressways; they are being built only now. You shared the roads with buses, trucks, three-wheelers, bicycles, pedestrians, bullock carts, cows, goats, and dogs. These days, there are more vehicles on the road than ever, including thousands of little three-wheelers swerving anywhere there is a gap in the traffic, but the roads have stayed the same size.

A few years ago, we were vacationing on the Caribbean island of Guadalupe, which is very mountainous. We had rented a car, a standard shift. When we collected the car at the airport, our son looks anxiously at me and asks, "Dad, are you sure you can handle this?" He has never seen me drive a stick shift. So I tell him, "Watch and learn", and off we go. At the end of that vacation, he tells me, "You need to teach me to drive a standard."

My father maintained the Anglia mostly by himself. The term "himself" is used loosely here as Asoka, Vasantha, and I were press-ganged into helping him. As he put it firmly to me, "If you want to drive, you need to understand the car first." The normal practice in Sri Lanka those days was that anything you could fix, you did yourself. My dad took this to an extreme and in his infinite wisdom decided that he would do most of the maintenance of the car without the help of a mechanic. He had the repair manual for the Anglia, a set of simple tools, and the muscle power of three teenage boys. He was ready to do battle with the car.

Over the years we dismantled and put back in working order pretty much everything in that car. We did the brakes many times, the suspension system, the steering mechanism, and much more. I could service and tune a carburetor before I even knew how the darn thing worked. We have unbolted and removed the engine from the car without using any special tools or lift mechanisms. Just unbolt the engine from the mounts, put ropes around it hanging from strong wooden poles, and lift it clear! If we had owned turning machines like lathes, I am sure my father would have even attempted to machine the parts.

One thing we had going for us was that cars those days were all mechanical with only a few electrical parts. They contained no electronics at all. So maintenance was all mechanical: just follow the instructions in the repair manual. We did not think too much about what we were doing at that time, but looking back I must say that these activities gave me a real sense of self-confidence in using my hands. They also gave me the ability to think logically. Vasantha still says that all the work on that car gave him a nice base on which he built his career as an aircraft maintenance engineer.

My father had the Anglia for more than thirty years. He decided to sell it after he started losing concentration while driving and had a minor accident. I am certain that it is still around, by now refurbished and rebuilt several times. Or did it fly back to England and audition for a small part in a certain movie? One wonders.

School Daze

There Is a School That Was Built for Me...

When we first moved to Mount Lavinia, the question was which school I would attend. At first this was not a problem as I was in kindergarten and I could go to any school for lower grades. So, I went to the same school that my sister attended, the Girl's High School. This was essentially a school for girls from Grades 1 to 12, but in early grades they accepted both girls and boys.

The issue was where next. In Colombo and in other major cities, the schools are segregated by gender, some exclusively for boys and others for girls. Mount Lavinia did not have a school for middle-class boys except the exclusive and private S. Thomas' College, which was run by the Anglican Church. Although it is considered one of the best boys schools in the country, my father did not want to send me there. He must have thought that after working so hard in the government's school takeover program it would be hypocritical of him to send me to a private school. The next option was to go to a boys school in Colombo. Given his position in the Education Service, he could have got me in to one of the several leading boys schools there. He did not like that on two accounts: one, it would be a longer commute from the Mount to Colombo for me, and two, being straight and honest, he did not like to use his official position to get me into a prominent school. One of my mother's most common grumblings was "Your father will never lift a finger to help you or your sister, but he is happy to help others."

So, what did he do? He created a brand new school for me in Mount Lavinia. There was a need for such a school in the area, and by creating a new school he would solve my schooling problem also. He got hold of the local Buddhist priest, Ven. Mapalagama Vipulasara, who was a powerful person in the country at that time and had lots of political clout, and a couple of other local businessmen, and started a primary school for boys. Working for the Education Department, where he had a strong reputation as an honest and efficient officer, it was not a problem for him to get resources assigned to a new school. Hena Road Junior Secondary School, as it was known, was started at a temporary location at the local temple in 1962 or '63. The school started with about 100 local kids. I was the first to be registered, with the student number 1. My father searched through the system and found some really good teachers and a brilliant principal, Mr. Wijayapala, who had been a friend of his from his teaching days. I am in an exclusive club: not many can claim that they had a school started just for them!

After that initial modest beginning, the school moved to its current premises with proper buildings, playgrounds, and other facilities. Given my father's special interest, the school grew rapidly and within a few years got a reputation as an excellent primary. It really fulfilled a need that was lacking in that area. The school that started with about 100 students now has over 3,000. We had a strong reputation for specializing in arts, dance, and music. In those years we participated in many arts festivals and won lots of accolades. I played drums in the school band. The school had a massive garden where the students grew vegetables that they sold to the surrounding community. The teachers were the absolute best — unforgettable characters that really shaped our young lives. I did not realize it then, but my father's influence on my life is incalculable.

It is kind of ironic that the school, which is thriving now, has been renamed after a late local politician that had nothing to do with creating or nurturing the institution. So the Hena Road Primary School I grew up with is now Lalith Athulathmudali College. My sister told me that none of the founding members were even mentioned at the ceremony that was held to rename the school. Most of them were still alive and living in the area at that time. My sister feels that our father was heartbroken that no acknowledgement was given to the people who were there at the beginning. But he was not one to complain. He did not say a word. In fact, he never even mentioned the school again.

In 2018 we were visiting Mount Lavinia and we had invited Buddhist priests to my sister's place to bless our ailing mother. On that particular day my brother-in-law and I went to the temple to fetch the priests to the house. This is the same temple where I started school all those years ago. While we were waiting for the priests to get ready, we were chatting with the current head priest of the temple. My brother-in-law introduced me to him, telling him that I was the first student of Hena Road Primary that started there with Ven. Vipulasara's help. During our conversation I told him that my journey that started there in Grade 1 in that temple ended with a PhD in engineering at the University of Toronto in Canada. I was not boasting, but just acknowledging something that had to be acknowledged. The priest told me that if I still had my original registration documents, report cards, or other related memorabilia, he would be happy to display them at the temple as a part of its history.

My Life at Thurstan College

At the end of Grade 5 my parents started to think about the next step for me. Hena Road Primary went only up to Grade 6 and my mother was insistent that we needed to find the next school for me sooner rather than waiting until I finished Grade 6.

In 1966 my father was in Australia at the University of Sydney on a scholarship arranged between the two governments. Without him around, my mother got really worried that I might not get a proper school to go to in Grade 7. So, she talked to a few of my father's friends in the Education Department and as a result I was asked to sit for an entrance examination at Thurstan College in Colombo, a school that would allow me to progress from Grade 6 to university.

At that time Thurstan College was not in the top tier of boys schools in Colombo, but my mother acting alone did not have the clout to approach the leading schools like Royal, Ananda, and Nalanda. I am pretty sure if we had waited for my father to return back to Sri Lanka, he would have found me a place in any government school that he liked, but my mother was panicking. So, I ended up at Thurstan College, a choice that I have never regretted. But this question has come up many a times later because people have asked "Your dad was a big shot at Education in those days. How come you went to Thurstan?" Well, that is how come.

I went to Thurstan College from 1966 to '72. In North American terms these would be my middle and high school years. Whereas I had been at the top of my class at Hena Road, scoring heavily in all of the courses and walking away with most of the class prizes awarded every year, I was a pretty middle-of-the road student at Thurstan. I suppose that's what happens when you move from a small pond to a bigger one.

One drastic change that happened when I moved to Thurstan College was how I got to the school every day. Hena Road Primary was within walking distance from our house; Thurstan is in Colombo, a bus ride away. In fact, I had to take two buses. I would take the local bus in the morning to the Mount Junction and then get on the school bus that was exclusive for Thurstan students. Each big school in Colombo had its own set of school buses for their own students. Travelling in the school buses was an adventure in itself. Because the same bunch of students from Mount Lavinia took the school bus everyday, over the years we developed a sense of camaraderie. The school bus was ours and was part of our identity as Thurstan students. These school buses were old City of London red double-deckers, and the upper deck was our castle. Things got interesting when we passed a bus of a rival school. All kinds of insults, taunts, and trash talk would be hurled from bus to bus. Standing up for our school loomed large in our minds and we would take no trash-talking from anyone without retaliation.

Things got really heated during the school cricket season because we flew our school flags from the buses. It was mayhem if two rival school buses flying school flags got stuck in traffic beside each other. Paper balls, folded paper "bullets" fired using rubberbands, small objects, anything that could be thrown would fly and water pistols filled with coloured water would be aimed at the rival bus, which would end up sprayed all over. Most of the time it was just the plain fun of boys being boys. Occasionally things got out of hand and the bus would stop on the side of the road till everyone settled down. On rare occasions, both buses were driven to the nearest police station by the exasperated drivers to calm the students down. It was indeed a brave bus driver who would attempt to overtake a flag-draped rival school bus during the cricket season.

School cricket was a matter of life and death to us. The cricket season starts in January and ends in March or April. Most schools in the big towns of Colombo, Kandy, and Galle would play each other at least once with the season culminating in a series of big matches, where each school had a designated rival to play the final game of the season against. One such big match encounter between Royal College in Colombo and S. Thomas' College in Mount Lavinia is now in its 140th year of playing. The game has been played continually every year except for a stoppage during World War II. The Royal-Thomian, as it is called, is considered to be the oldest uninterrupted sports rivalry between two schools in the world. Every year the game easily attracts 30,000 to 40,000 spectators. The alumni of the two schools who live abroad are known to plan their vacations back in Sri Lanka to include the game.

In not quite as long-standing a rivalry, Thurstan College plays Isipathana College in our big match, and that series has now been played for more than fifty years.

In addition to cricket, rugby is also taken very seriously in Sri Lanka. With my beanpole-like physical stature there was no question of me playing rugby, but in my high school days my friends and I used to go to a lot of rugby matches. I enjoy both sports, cricket with its cerebral nature, requiring strategies and planning, and the raw, physical nature of rugby.

Getting back to the academic part of my high school life, the classes at Thurstan were pretty uninspiring, the teachers were overworked, and they felt and looked tired, with a couple of exceptions. It was a drag to get through the school year. The only exception was the music program. As I explained earlier, I was "volunteered" for the school orchestra by my father. It had just been formed under the new music teacher Mr. Yogananda. We had our sights on the inter-school competition that year. Mr. Yogananda composed the music and we practised like demons. This was when we were in Grade 7 and 8. One good thing about orchestra practice was that we were allowed to get out of our regular classes to practise. The bad thing was that we had practices every day after school hours, and sometimes on Saturdays. We could not say no. Mr. Yogananda had a terrible temper if his players missed practice times and we were deathly scared of him. But the music he composed for us was divine. I can still remember the melodies and even now sometimes I hum them to myself, prompting our son to ask me what I am humming. As explained earlier, all those practices paid off big time and we stormed the competition and won the inter-school championship that year. Nobody knew where we had come from, the orchestra having been formed only the previous year. However, I think no one in our orchestra ever thought that we would not win.

After Grade 8 things get serious in Sri Lankan schools. Grades 9 and 10 are preparation for the first nationwide examination that is conducted by the government to determine if you are qualified to advance to Grades 11 and 12 where your courses are specific to what you will study at university. So basically, what you are going to be for the rest of your life is determined at the end of Grade 10 when you sit for the General Certificate of Education (GCE) Ordinary Level exams. You take eight subjects and are required to attain a minimum qualifying standard. You do not get numerical marks but are given an Ordinary, Credit, or Distinction level pass for each subject.

My time in Grade 9 and 10 is a blur. I knew what I had to do to get through the GCE O-level and I just did it without really thinking about what I was studying. It was just a matter of digesting the material, reviewing, practising, and memorizing. In some subjects, particularly in chemistry and math, I had extra tutoring. You finished your Grade 10, sat for the exam, and anxiously waited for a couple of months for the results to be announced.

A few incidents and two teachers stand out from my Grade 9 and 10 years. One was Mr. Zoysa, who was our class master and biology teacher, nominally in charge of us, and the other was Mr. Wijedasa, who taught us math.

Mr. Zoysa was one of the most interesting teachers that I have ever met. He was a great storyteller. He had just returned to the island from a tour of Western universities and schools and was full of stories of where he had been and what he had seen. In most of his classes, half the time he spent just telling stories, hardly related to the curriculum. We all loved to hear these stories, and he was one of the teachers that we grudgingly respected.

Our Grade 10 class was a riot. There were all kinds of characters up to all kinds of pranks. I remember one day the class was without a teacher, and things became unruly and noisy. We were spinning metal plates across the classroom in frisbee fashion with lots of shouting, noise, and cheering. Some teacher in an adjoining classroom must have complained, because Mr. Zoysa came storming into our class. He must have been told that his class was out of control.

Unfortunately for me, right at that instance I'm the only one standing up and getting ready to frisbee a metal plate across the room. Talk about timing. He storms in, we all freeze. I am caught like a deer in a beam of light.

"What the devil are you guys doing? What is that in your hand?"

"Sir, it's a flying saucer", someone chimes in from the back of the class. Mr. Zoysa looks wild. "Tantirige, come here", he says menacingly. I go forward reluctantly. He looks at me, not saying a thing. *Whack!* A thundering slap lands across my face. "Go back to your seat."

I get back to my chair. My face is stinging from the slap, but I can't show pain, under any circumstances; no tears. Be brave; act normal. The class is now deathly quiet. Then Mr. Zoysa goes on this long talk. He tells us he had heard how unruly we are, how bad our behaviour is, and how disappointed he is in all of us. It is pretty upsetting to listen to, especially coming from a teacher that we somewhat respect. Then he picks up our list of names and tells us, "OK, I am going to predict the future of every one of you jokers right now." So he goes through the list, calling each name one by one and describing what he thinks of each one of us and what our future will be based on what he knows about us. Down the list he goes, and he comes to my name. "Tantirige." He shakes his head sadly. "I had expected great things from you. Unfortunately, you are not going to amount to anything."

That is not the end of this story. A few years later Mr. Zoysa's brother married my sister. They had met while studying in Moscow. When they got married in 1977, I was in university studying engineering. I had it all planned: at the wedding, I was going to look him straight in the eye and ask, "What do you think of me now? Not amounting to anything, eh?"

As he walked into the wedding reception, he sees me and walks straight to me. He looks at me and without batting an eye says, "Remember that slap I gave you all those years ago? That is when you turned things around." He turns and walks off. Talk about having the last word. That was Mr. Zoysa, my brother-in-law's elder brother.

The other teacher that I remember distinctly after all these years is Mr. Wijedasa, our math teacher in Grades 9 and 10. He was a terror, but was excellent at teaching math. He had this habit where he would ask questions in a rapid-fire fashion, going from one student to the other without giving us much time to think. If you missed an answer you had to get up and stand on your chair. So after the first round of questions, half the class is standing on their chairs. But he doesn't stop: he starts again from the top of the list with more questions for the students who are still seated. This would go on until the whole class was standing on their chairs. Then he would look at us in a particular manner, smile, shrug his shoulders, and walk away.

Despite all the craziness that went on, we completed Grade 10, and in December of 1970 sat for the island-wide GCE O-level exam. I was not sure I had put in enough work to prepare for the exam. So I was more than surprised when the results were released a couple of months later. I had done well, nowhere near the top but well above minimum requirements to progress to Grade 11 and 12. What made people stand up and notice was that while I had Credit passes for seven of the eight subjects that I sat for, I failed in Buddhism. My friends thought I had made history. As one remarked, "This makes you perfect for the priesthood."

Usually Buddhism is one of the easy subjects in the set of eight and most students managed to pass it without too much difficulty. You got indoctrinated in Buddhism from a young age at home, at the temple, and at school, so you were not supposed to fail an exam in Buddhism. I was not surprised at the results because I hated learning by memorization, which is what religious studies usually are. My parents, who were not deeply religious, simply did not care. In their thinking, I had got through GCE O-level and that was what mattered. My grandma on the other hand, who was very religious, shook her head sadly and said, "Ayoo son, I always wished that you would pass Buddhism with a Distinction."

"Look, *Archchi*", I retorted, "even Lord Buddha would have failed if he took that exam."

With that first hurdle out of the way, I had to get ready for the next step: the GCE Advance Level examination in two years' time. This is one of the most important events in a student's life as it is the university entrance selection exam. This was a real ball-breaker, with less than five per cent of the students taking the exam getting a spot in university at that time; the numbers for engineering and medicine were even smaller. For the GCE A-level, you take only four subjects. With the intention of studying engineering or sciences, I had pure mathematics, applied mathematics, physics, and chemistry. The study material was extensive and exhaustive, and covered both Grade 11 and 12. In addition to the study material, students taking physics, chemistry, or biology courses had lab work. As a rule, pretty much everyone taking science streams had extra tutoring.

As we got more and more into Grade 11, I became uneasy. I felt that the teachers were not taking much interest in preparing students for the coming exams. Many times, the teachers who were supposed to be in class were not there, and students just wasted the time sitting around chatting. In addition, school cricket season was in full swing and a number of my class friends were on the cricket team, so we spent a lot of time talking cricket. By the end of Grade 11, I was in panic mode. We had not covered even a fraction of the material that we should have, and looking at past exam questions it was obvious to me that I did not have a clue.

I went to my father and told him what was going on. He was pretty disturbed; after all, he was a senior Education Officer in charge of the schools! After some thought, he asked me if I wanted to leave Thurstan and join a private college that specialized in prepping students for GCE A-level exams. That was a tough decision for me. I would be leaving all my friends that I had known since Grade 6. There were a lot of memories associated with that school. My time with the orchestra, cricket matches, antics on the school bus, and other crazy stuff that we did. I was also worried about tuition fees. Specialized private schools' tuition fees were high, and I was not sure if my parents could afford that. I told my dad, "But you don't have the money for me to go to this place." He replied, "I will worry about the money, you worry about the studies."

So, I left Thurstan College and joined Aquinas College, a private college in Colombo run by the Catholic Church preparing students for various professions. They had recently started a GCE A-level prep course. Aquinas was a totally different experience for me from school; it was more like being on a university campus. For the first time I was in coed classes that had both boys and girls. It was kind of neat being able to sit in the cafeteria in groups that included both males and females and argue about a complex math problem or talk about the latest movie opening. The teaching was very good, and for the first time I began to feel optimistic about getting through to university.

On the other hand, I was not happy about the financial strain that I was putting my parents through. Unlike in Western countries, there was no tradition in Sri Lanka of students doing part-time work to pay for their education, so instead I was absolutely determined that I would study as hard as I could and ace the exams. Those eighteen or so months that I spent studying and prepping for the GCE A-level probably constituted the most intense time in my life. There was just one focus, and that was to study and prepare for the exams. The only time I would take a break from studies was in the evenings. I would go out and hang out with my neighbourhood friends for a couple of hours at our old playground or on the Mount beach where we would sit and chat and watch the sunsets.

When we were not in classes, I had a friend that studied with me. His name was Lalith, and we two would study at our homes. On some days he would be at my place and at other times I would be at his place. Lalith, who became a fast friend of mine during this time, now lives in Australia. A couple of years ago he and his wife, Rohini, were passing through Toronto and we met for the first time in about forty years. We had a great time reminiscing about those days. We even remembered food we ate during those intense study sessions. "Do you remember the bathala* and lunu miris† that your mom used to prepare for us those days?" Of course we did; those memories will never fade away.

By the end of 1973, after eighteen months of backbreaking and brain-mushing work, I felt as ready as I ever could be for the exam. The only subject that I was not too confident about was chemistry, which had a significant amount of material that one had to memorize. Everything else was fine. We had done literally thousands of practice problems in math, physics, and chemistry so that we would not be surprised at the exam. When I walked into the exam hall that year, I was totally confident that I was going to ace it. Four days later I walked out having finished the last exam, knowing that I had aced it. It was a large monkey off my back. I could go home, look my father in the eyes and tell him, "Yes, it is done. Yes, I did well, but let's not count our chickens just yet. Let's wait for the results."

The GCE A-level results were announced a few months after the exams. As I expected, I had done really well. Looking at the results, I knew I would not have any problems in selecting any engineering or science course that I wanted to study at university. More than that, I had never forgotten my father's words, "I will worry about the money,

---

* Sweet yams.
† The fiery Sri Lankan concoction of chilies, onions, salt and lemon, ground to a paste and sprinkled with bits of Maldive fish. Its alternate name is "dynamite".

you worry about the studies." He had kept his word; I had kept my side of the bargain. That was more important that anything else to me.

I still remember the day the results came out. A bunch of us went to a movie to celebrate. It was a kind of a combined celebration and wake. In our group there were a few of us who were going on to university, and then there were others who had not met the requirements and would be repeating the exams a year later. The movie was The Poseidon Adventure and it was being shown at the Savoy Cinema in Wellawatta. We were a boisterous bunch and were noisy in the theatre, shouting rude comments at the characters on screen. Finally, the theatre manager comes to where we are seated and tells us, "If you boys don't pipe down and behave, I will have you thrown out." One of us replies back, "Please uncle, we are celebrating the A-level results. Some of us are going to university."

"If you don't behave son, it is not the university you will be going to!" he retorted. So, we piped down and behaved.

Some time later, my father returns home from work one day carrying a brand-new guitar. "This is for you for getting through to university." That is one of the most cherished gifts that I have ever received in my life.

This story ends with me entering the University of Moratuwa, one of the leading engineering schools on the island, in 1975 to study chemical engineering. I spent the next four years there. I had lots of fun during those years and along the way met my future wife, Kanthi. I completed the BASc in 1979, moved to Canada in 1980 to attend the University of Toronto, and a few years later finished up my university life with two more degrees, an MASc and a PhD in engineering. Kanthi and I got married in 1982 while we were still doing our graduate studies at the University of Toronto. It took a while, but in 1989 both Kanthi and I completed our PhDs and started to work. After all those university years, finally we could start our real life. Our son arrived a few years later. I feel that I spent way too much time in universities wasting my life.

Well, that last paragraph covers a lot of water under the bridge of life. In that story there are ups and downs, happiness, heartbreak, smiles, tears, times that were as high as the Everest and lows as low as the Mariana Trench, the whole works. Adult life is much more complicated than a child's life. It is not yet the time to write that story.

My Canadian journey has a few more kilometres to go. The end is not yet known, so the story will have to wait.

Just What Did You Do for Me, Dad?

In the summer of 1999, just before he suddenly passed away, my father and mother stayed at our house in Toronto for a few months. It was their first time in Canada, and an opportunity for them to interact with our son who by then was four years old, as well as an opportunity for me to treat my parents to a nice time for the first time in my life. Nineteen years after I left their house, finally I could welcome them to a house of my own.

During their stay they visit my office, and I show my dad my PhD thesis. He flips through it, a thick document on complex fluid mechanics and says, "I don't understand any of this." I tell him, "Well, it might be a big consolation for you to know that even I don't understand most of it, and I wrote the darn thing!"

Although he did not understand a word of my thesis, I hope it gave him a moment to reflect on all that he had done for me. I don't think I ever said to him, "Thank you, Dad, for what you did."

If we Buddhists had tombstones for our dead, those words would be on his stone.

Coming Back Full Circle

It is August 2018 and we have been in Sri Lanka for two weeks. This is the last day of our visit. Later tonight we are flying back to Toronto. Like all our visits to Sri Lanka these days, it has been a rushed two weeks. There are many things you have to do during such a visit: spend time with your mother, meet family obligations, visit ailing relatives, and participate in a wedding or two. Then, this being Sri Lanka, take some time off to go to the mountains and beaches. Amid all of this I really did not have that much time to visit the old house down Gothami Mavatha.

At the last moment, I got a chance for a quick visit to the old house. That is how I ended up walking down my old street that evening. I am glad that I at least had the short time at the house, for this might be the last time I will be here. We are planning to sell the house, as neither my sister nor I am in a position to keep it in good repair anymore. So, I go in, take a look around the house one final time, walk a bit in the garden, and take a few photos.*

Later that night as I wait for our flight at Colombo airport, I begin to go through all the photos that I took

---

* As this book was going to print, the news came from Sri Lanka that our old house on Gothami Mavatha has been sold. The beloved house with so many memories is no longer ours. May it stand for many more years, providing a home, shelter, refuge, and a place of many happy memories to another family and a new set of children.

during the visit. As I come to the set of photos that I took at Gothami Mavatha, time seems to stand still. My mind goes back nearly fifty years to a different place and a different time. As in the famous movie line, it was "a long time ago in a galaxy far, far away".

As I look through the photos, I see more than what I recorded through my camera. My life is flashing like a movie reel on high speed. I see the house as it was, when it was a place full of life, laughter, and people. I hear my sister singing along to a song on the radio. I see my cousins hanging out on the veranda playing cards. I see the old Ford Anglia parked in the driveway. I see Ringo prowling in the garden. Then I see the house as it is now. Old, tired, and lonely. The veranda is empty, the windows are all closed. The fruit trees that adorned the garden once are all gone except for the old mango tree that my father planted many, many years ago. Tears come to my eyes. As Buddhists we should not feel sad. "Everything is impermanent", I say to myself, but it still hurts.

As I look at the photos, the house is talking to me. It is an old man. He is pleased that I have come to visit him one last time. He seems to read my mind and ask me questions. Do you remember the first time you moved into your room when I was new? Do you remember that road cricket game where you scored 91 runs, your highest score anywhere? Do you remember the joy of getting the university entrance results and realizing that you had scored enough marks to study engineering? Do you remember the violin lessons and your music teacher who came to the house? Do you remember picking up a guitar for the first time and going through the chords belting out "Let It Be"? Do you remember dancing to the tunes of Bollywood with your cousins? Do you remember the loneliness you felt when your sister went abroad to study? Do you remember the night you left the country for Canada?

Did you know then that you would never come back to Gothami Mavatha to live? Do you remember the first time you brought your then seven-month-old son to the house to find your old crib set up for him in your old room? How much do you remember and how much have you forgotten?

"If only walls could talk", I think.

"I am talking to you", says the house.

"But soon you will be gone", say I.

"Don't feel sad", says the house. "Walls may crumble, roofs may fall, trees may die, but memories will remain."

God, what memories they are.

Epilogue

I want to end this with a verse from a Sinhala song that I love:

සඳක් බැස ගියා අවරගිරේ, ඉරක් උදා කරලා
මටත් ලොවක් තිබුණා මතකයි මම ඉඳී සිහි කරලා
දෙළුම් මල් පිපුණු දෙවැට දිගේ පාසල් ගිය කාලේ
මල් වගේ සිනාසුණු කෙල්ලන් හා මතකයි මගේ බාලේ

A rough translation, which does not do justice to the original, goes like this:

> As the moon was setting in the west
> And the sun was about to break free
> I stood reminiscing one early dawn
> About a world that was once part of me
>
> There was a road with flowering pomegranate trees
> Along which I walked to my school
> With girls that smiled like those flowers
> I will always remember, those enchanting days

By the late and great Clarance Wijewardena
Composer, singer, and guitar player extraordinaire

Acknowledgements

No work of this nature is just your own, and there are a number of people that need to be acknowledged. First of all, all those people who were part of my life in those crazy and enchanting days in Sri Lanka and who are now unwitting characters in this story. Thank you for making my life interesting.

A very special mention here of my wife Kanthi and our son Sanjay, who have shared my life, in its glory and its ups and downs, for such a long time. You two have been the greatest teachers that I have had in this life. You gave space for me and made it possible for me to think about my past and write it down.

Then there are a number of others who made significant contributions to this story. The first is my sister, Mala, who when I first mentioned that I was thinking of writing this memoir gave me all kinds of encouragement. She also read one of the earlier versions of what I had written and reminded me of things that I had forgotten. Thanks are also due to those of my extended family in Sri Lanka who read and "vetted" the book.

A huge thank you to my "Canadian crew", my coworkers: Mei Tamkei, Holly Gardiner, Keith Weaver, and John Lotoski. They read this story from a non-Sri Lankan perspective and offered invaluable suggestions that have made this what it is. They pointed out what was missing and what was confusing to non-Sri Lankan readers. John, in true engineer fashion, did an amazingly detailed review pointing out inconsistencies in different parts of the story. Keith, in addition to reading the manuscript, kindly guided me through the intricate world of book publishing.

I would also like to thank Iguana Books for their efforts: Greg Ioannou, who first saw my manuscript in its very raw form and decided that it was good enough for publication; Toby Keymer, who did wonders with me in editing (He seems to read my mind.); Holly Warren, who did the proofreading of the final version; and Meghan Behse, who did an amazing job with the cover designs. Thank you for making this whole process painless for a rookie.

I would be a remiss if I failed to mention a number of Sri Lankan authors who have published in English in recent times. Names like Michael Ondaatje, Shyam Selvadurai, and a host of others come to mind. They gave me the confidence that I could put down my thoughts in English rather than in my mother tongue. There are a number of great authors that are publishing in English in Sri Lanka at present and I wish they could get more exposure outside the country, particularly in the West so that more people can appreciate the breathtaking storytelling that happens on that small island of mine.

www.ingramcontent.com/pod-product-compliance
Lightning Source LLC
LaVergne TN
LVHW090116080426
835507LV00040B/910